Called to GLOBAL SOLIDARI✝Y

International Challenges for U.S. Parishes

A Statement of the
National Conference of Catholic Bishops
with Parish Resources

United States Catholic Conference • Washington, D.C.

The Committee on International Policy developed this statement, which was approved by the Administrative Board and considered by the full body of bishops. The statement and its appendix, the "Framework for Parish Global Solidarity," were approved by the bishops on November 12, 1997. Part II, "Suggestions for Action" and Part III, "Handouts and Resources" were produced to accompany the statement under the coordination of the Department of Social Development and World Peace, in collaboration with a number of conference offices and national Catholic organizations. They were approved by the chair of the International Policy Committee. The statement and appendices are approved for publication by the undersigned.

Monsignor Dennis M. Schnurr
General Secretary
NCCB/USCC

Photographs: CNS/James Baca (lower right cover; p. 7), CNS/Martin Lueders (lower left cover; facing p.1), CNS/Barb Fraze (upper left cover; p. 24), CNS/KNA (upper right cover; p. 12).

Scripture texts used in this work are taken from the *New American Bible,* copyright © 1991, 1986, and 1970 by the Confraternity of Christian Doctrine, Washington, DC 20017 and are used by permission of copyright owner. All rights reserved.

ISBN 1-57455-118-3

First Printing, February 1998

Dear Pastors and Parish Leaders:

Some of the most compelling, and often most difficult, challenges facing our Church and our nation are the poverty and injustices experienced by our brothers and sisters around the world. Our Lord's message of love for our neighbors requires us not to turn away from the complexity of these problems but to respond with generosity and hope. This is a challenge for every Catholic parish and every Catholic believer.

In November 1997, the U.S. bishops issued a statement on our international obligations titled *Called to Global Solidarity: International Challenges for U.S. Parishes.* It recognizes the many outstanding efforts of U.S. parishes to address the needs of people overseas. It also challenges each of us to consider what we are already doing and to try to do more. As the bishops point out,

> A suffering world must find a place in the pastoral priorities of every Catholic parish. . . . A parish's "catholicity" is illustrated in its willingness to go beyond its own boundaries to extend the Gospel, serve those in need, and work for global justice and peace. . . . This solidarity is expressed in our prayer and stewardship, how we form our children and invest our resources, and the choices we make at work and in the public arena. . . . A central task for the next century will be building families of faith that reach out beyond national boundaries.

The following "Suggestions for Action" were developed to help parishes act on the message of *Called to Global Solidarity*. Rather than suggesting entirely new parish programs, they offer concrete, practical ideas for incorporating international concerns into existing parish ministries. The "Handouts and Resources" are intended to be copied, distributed among appropriate staff and leaders, and adapted to fit the unique opportunities in each parish.

This resource includes the following sections, which may be copied and distributed to parish leaders:

- How to Get Started
- Assessment Questions
- Anchoring Solidarity: Prayer, Worship, and Preaching
- Teaching Solidarity: Education and Formation
- Living Solidarity: Work, Family, and Citizenship
- Investing in Solidarity: Stewardship
- Practicing Solidarity: Outreach and Charity
- Promoting Solidarity: Advocacy and Political Responsibility
- Handouts and Resources

There is also a companion video, *Global Solidarity*, which can be a useful starting point for parish councils, social concerns committees, educational programs, and other groups. The video can be ordered by calling 800-235-8722.

I hope these suggestions and resources will be helpful as your parish examines, strengthens, and builds on its current efforts to promote global solidarity. I encourage you to copy them, adjust them, and use them in whatever way you would find most helpful. Finally, I thank you for all you are doing to act on the gospel message of justice and peace.

Sincerely,

+ Theodore E. McCarrick

Most Reverend Theodore E. McCarrick, chair
International Policy Committee
Archbishop of Newark

Acknowledgments

The contributions of the following organizations and individuals to Part II of this document are gratefully acknowledged:

USCC Department of Social Development and World Peace
Catholic Relief Services
USCC Migration and Refugee Services
Catholic Near East Welfare Association
NCCB Committee on World Mission
NCCB Office to Aid the Church in Central and Eastern Europe
NCCB Secretariat for Latin America
Society for the Propagation of the Faith
Dr. Ron Pagnucco and Bryan Pelino, Mount St. Mary's College

Table of Contents

PART I

Called to Global Solidarity: International Challenges for U.S. Parishes

Introduction

At a time of dramatic global changes and challenges, Catholics in the United States face special responsibilities and opportunities. We are members of a universal Church that transcends national boundaries and calls us to live in solidarity and justice with the peoples of the world. We are also citizens of a powerful democracy with enormous influence beyond our borders. As Catholics and Americans we are uniquely called to global solidarity.

One of God's greatest gifts is the universal character of the Church, blessing and calling us to live in solidarity with our sisters and brothers in faith. In many ways our community of faith practices solidarity every day. Missionaries preach the Gospel and celebrate the eucharist. Catholic relief workers feed the hungry and promote development. Our prayers, donations, and volunteers assist the Church in Latin America, Central and Eastern Europe, Asia, and Africa. The United States Catholic Conference and other Catholic groups defend human life and human rights, promote global justice, and pursue peace.

However, these international institutions, programs, and collections have not yet awakened a true sense of solidarity among many Catholics in the United States. The international commitment of the Church in the United States is not all it can and should be. Our parishes often act as islands of local religious activity rather than as parts of the mystical body of Christ. At the parish level, where the Church lives, we need to integrate more fully the international dimensions of Catholic discipleship within a truly universal Church.

While many parishes do build global bridges, the Church's teaching on global solidarity is too often unknown, unheard, or unheeded. The coming jubilee offers U.S. parishes a graced moment to strengthen our international solidarity, since the themes of the millennium call us so clearly to this vital task.

The Church's teaching on international justice and peace is not simply a mandate for a few large agencies, but a challenge for every believer and every Catholic community of faith. The demands of solidarity require not another program, but greater awareness and integration into the ongoing life of the parish. The Church's universal character can be better reflected in how every parish prays, educates, serves, and acts. A parish reaching beyond its own members and beyond national boundaries is a truly "catholic" parish. An important role for the parish is to challenge and encourage every believer to greater global solidarity.

These reflections are intended for pastors, parish leaders, and other involved Catholics. They address the Catholic call to global solidarity in two distinct but related ways. One is the individual responsibility of every Catholic founded in our baptism and expressed in our everyday choices and actions. Another is the essential role of the parish as the spiritual home and religious resource for the Christian faithful, both sacramental and educational, and as a place for common prayer and action in pursuit of global solidarity.

> **A parish reaching beyond its own members and beyond national boundaries is a truly "catholic" parish.**

A few years ago we developed and adopted *Communities of Salt and Light,* a modest reflection on the social mission of the parish. We would like to build on the remarkable response to this document and encourage parishes to strengthen ties of solidarity with all the peoples of the world, especially the poor and persecuted. We also wish to provide a framework for parish leaders looking to strengthen or initiate programs of international solidarity.

Signs of the Times

For Catholics in the United States, the call to international solidarity takes on special urgency. We live in the largest of the world's wealthy nations, a global military and political power. Yet all around us are signs of suffering and need:

- 35,000 persons die of hunger and its consequences every day around the world.
- The specter of genocide and ethnic violence has become sadly familiar in Central Africa and other places.
- Christian and other believers are persecuted or harassed in China, Vietnam, Indonesia, parts of the Middle East, and within our own hemisphere.
- Conflicts with religious dimensions divide and destroy people in Bosnia, Sudan, Northern Ireland, East Timor, and too many other places.

MIGRATION AND REFUGEE SERVICES

On behalf of the bishops in the United States, Migration and Refugee Services (MRS) works through more than one hundred dioceses to welcome, care for, and integrate newcomers into U.S. society. MRS welcomes Catholic newcomers into the Church, educates Americans to respect diverse cultures, and promotes justice, compassion, and respect for the dignity of every person. As one of the oldest and largest private resettlement agencies in the world, MRS promotes policies and services to meet the pastoral and human needs of migrants, immigrants, refugees, asylum seekers, displaced persons, and other people on the move through its pastoral care, refugee programs, and policy units. Contact:

Migration and Refugee Services
United States Catholic Conference
3211 Fourth Street, N.E.
Washington, DC 20017-1194
Telephone: 202-541-3352
Fax: 202-541-3399
E-mail: cphan@nccbuscc.org

- Foreign debt crushes hopes and paralyzes progress in too many poor nations.
- Refugees and displaced persons are overwhelming borders in much of the world.
- 26,000 people, mostly civilians, are maimed or killed every year by antipersonnel landmines.
- Forests, rivers, and other parts of God's creation are being destroyed by environmental neglect and devastation.
- Some nations and nongovernmental organizations resort to attacks on human life, including coerced abortion and sterilization.

These are just some examples of the crisis of solidarity facing our world.

Our world has changed dramatically. Walls have fallen and communism has collapsed. Lech Walesa, Vaclav Havel, and Nelson Mandela have moved from prison cells to presidential offices. The Cold War has ended, but our world is still haunted by too much violence and not enough development for those in need.

During the last decade, the rapid globalization of markets, communication, and transportation has dramatically drawn the world together. Global economic forces empower some and impoverish many. The gulf between rich and poor nations has widened, and the sense of responsibility toward the world's poor and oppressed has grown weaker. The world watched for too long as thousands died in Bosnia, Rwanda, and Zaire.

There is increasing complacency about the defense of human rights. Our country is tempted to turn its back on long traditions of openness and hospitality to immigrants and refugees who have nowhere to turn.

The United States ranks first in the world in the weapons we sell to poor nations yet near last in the proportion of our resources we devote to development for the poor.

Our nation is deeply affected by economic, political, and social forces around the globe. The effects of these forces are evident in our economy, the immigrants and refugees among us, the threat of terrorism, dynamics of the drug trade, and pressures on workers. We are tempted by the illusion of isolationism to turn away from global leadership in an understandable but dangerous preoccupation with the problems of our own communities and nation. In the face of these challenges we see divergent paths. One path is that of indifference, even hostility to global

PROPAGATION OF THE FAITH

The Society for the Propagation of the Faith fosters the universal missionary spirit of the Church, sensitizing Catholics to the universal implication of their baptism into Christ. Through World Mission Sunday, the Propagation of the Faith encourages prayer, collects funds, and catechizes on the mission-ary dimension of the Catholic faith. Through the Missionary Cooperation Plan, missionaries speak in parishes. In a wide variety of written and audiovisual materials, the Propagation of the Faith focuses on the proclamation of the Gospel, the building up of the Church, and authentic human development. Contact:

Your Diocesan Director for
Propagation of the Faith
(or The Society for the
Propagation of the Faith)
366 Fifth Avenue
New York, NY 10001
Telephone: 800-431-2222
Fax: 212-563-8725
Website: www.propfaith.org

engagement. Another path views the world as simply a global market for the goods and services of the United States.

Our faith calls us to a different road—a path of global responsibility and solidarity. The call to solidarity is at the heart of Pope John Paul II's leadership. He has insisted that the test of national leadership is how we reach out to defend and enhance the dignity of the

poor and vulnerable, at home and around the world. He calls us to defense of all human life and care for God's creation. In his visits to this country, the Holy Father called on our nation to "spare no effort in advancing authentic freedom and in fostering human rights and solidarity."

Theological Foundations

The Moral Challenge

Cain's question, "Am I my brother's keeper?" (Gn 4:9), has global implications and is a special challenge for our time, touching not one brother but all our sisters and brothers. Are we responsible for the fate of the world's poor? Do we have duties to suffering people in far-off places? Must we respond to the needs of suffering refugees in distant nations? Are we keepers of the creation for future generations? For the followers of Jesus, the answer is yes. Indeed, we are our brothers' and sisters' keepers. As mem-bers of God's one human family, we acknowledge our duties to people in far-off places. We accept God's charge to care for all human life and for all creation.

We have heard the Lord's command, "Love your neighbor as yourself." In our linked and limited world, loving our neighbor has global implications. In faith, we know our neighbors live in Rwanda and Sudan, in East Timor and China, in Bosnia and Central America, as well as across our country and next door. Baptism, confirmation, and continuing participation in the body of Christ call us to action for "the least among us" without regard for boundaries or borders.

One Human Family

Beyond differences of language, race, ethnicity, gen-der, culture, and nation, we are one human family. Whether at World Youth Day, on World Mission Sunday, or in the daily celebration of the liturgy, the Church gathers people of every nation, uniting them in worship of the one God who is maker and redeemer of all. In so doing, the Church attests to the God-given unity of the human family and the human calling to build community.

Promoting the unity of the human family is the task of the whole Church. It belongs to the Holy Father, but it also belongs to the local parish. In the eucharist the Church prays for the peace of the world and the growth of the Church in love, and it advances these gifts. Readings from Acts and the Letters of Paul tell us of the concern of distant churches for the needy communities in Jerusalem and Macedonia. In faith, the world's hungry and homeless, the victims of injustice and religious persecution, are not mere issues; they are our sisters and brothers.

The Demands of Solidarity

Pope John Paul II has written, "Sacred Scripture con-tinually speaks to us of an active commitment to our neighbor and demands of us a shared responsibility for all of humanity. This duty is not limited to one's own family, nation or state, but extends progressively to all . . . so no one can consider himself extraneous or indifferent to the lot of another member of the human family" (*Centesimus Annus* [CA], no. 51).

Duties of solidarity and the sacrifices they entail fall not just on individuals but on groups and nations as well (CA, no. 51; *Populorum Progressio,* no. 48). According to Pope John Paul II, solidarity with the human family consists in "a firm and persevering determination to commit oneself to the common good" (*Sollicitudo Rei Socialis,* no. 38). In pursuit of solidarity, Pope John Paul II calls for a worldwide effort to promote development, an effort that "involves sacrificing the positions of income and of power enjoyed by the more developed economies" in the interest of "an overall human enrichment to the family of nations" (CA, no. 52).

Solidarity is action on behalf of the one human family, calling us to help overcome the divisions in our world. Solidarity binds the rich to the poor. It makes the free zealous for the cause of the oppressed. It drives the comfortable and secure to take risks for the victims of tyranny and war. It calls those who are strong to care for those who are weak and vulnerable across the spectrum of human life. It opens homes and hearts to those in flight from terror and to migrants whose daily toil supports affluent lifestyles. Peacemaking, as Pope John Paul II has told us, is the work of solidarity.

Pope John Paul II sharply challenges the growing gaps between rich and poor nations and between rich and poor within nations. He recognizes important values of market economics but insists that they be guided by the option for the poor and the principle of the global common good. He challenges leaders to respect human life and human rights, to protect workers and the vulnerable. He insists that nations halt the arms trade, ban landmines, promote true development, and relieve the crushing burden of international debt. The Holy Father's call to global responsibility is the core of a Catholic international agenda and the foundation of a Catholic commitment to solidarity.

U.S. Catholic Responses and Responsibilities

Around the United States, parishes, dioceses, and national church agencies strengthen the ties that bind our global family of faith. The U.S. Catholic community is a leader in global missions, relief, and devel-

opment efforts. Our missionaries and relief workers risk their lives to preach and act on the Gospel.

Catholic Relief Services is our community's international relief and development arm, offering the solidarity of the American Catholic community to people in more than eighty countries. Each year, the United States Catholic Conference's Migration and Refugee Services assists almost a third of the refugees who flee religious and political persecution and immigrants seeking a new life. Through annual collections, the Church in the United States provides financial and other support for the mission and pastoral programs of the Church in Latin America, Central and Eastern Europe, Asia, and Africa. Through the Propagation of the Faith we help preach the Gospel, aid missionaries, and support the development of local churches. Through the work of our International Policy Committee, the U.S. bishops advocate for the needs of the poor and vulnerable around the globe.

DEPARTMENT OF SOCIAL DEVELOPMENT AND WORLD PEACE

The USCC Department of Social Development and World Peace helps the U.S. bishops share Catholic social teaching, apply and advocate its principles on major international issues, and stand in solidarity with the Church in other parts of the world. Through its Office of International Justice and Peace, the bishops' conference develops policy and advocates on issues of global justice and peace, human rights and religious liberty, debt and development. Parishes use USCC statements, alerts, and other resources to reflect, educate, and act on international issues on their own or as participants in diocesan ministry and legislative activities. Contact:

Office of International Justice and Peace
United States Catholic Conference
3211 Fourth Street, N.E.
Washington, DC 20017-1194
Telephone: 202-541-3199
Fax: 202-541-3339
E-mail: Jhiatt-booker@nccbuscc.org
Website: www.nccbuscc.org/justice/sdwp

The international agencies of the U.S. bishops are working together to strengthen the international witness of the United States Catholic Conference and to help parishes recognize their responsibilities as parts of a universal Church. Accompanying this reflection are brief summaries of the work of these agencies and how parishes can reach them. There are many other examples of U.S. Catholic international commitment: the Holy Childhood Association, Catholic Near East Welfare Association, National Council of Catholic Women, mission societies, religious advocacy groups, volunteer programs, exchange programs, and thousands of other ties between our Catholic community and the Church in other lands. These efforts put the Gospel to work and change lives here and abroad.

Across the country parishes are building relationships with sister parishes, especially in Latin America but also in Africa, Eastern Europe, Asia, and Oceania. Parish committees and legislative networks respond to pleas for help and advocate on issues of development, human rights, and peace. Parishes honor the memories of martyrs in Central America and Africa, and they act in defense of the unborn, the hungry, migrants, and refugees. Human rights advocates work for the release of prisoners of conscience and those suffering for their faith. Many parishes work on an ecumenical and interfaith basis to build bridges and act effectively on issues of global solidarity. These commitments transform and enrich U.S. parishes. As bishops, we seek to fan these flames of charity and justice in our parishes, dioceses, and national structures, so that the Church in the United States will be better light for our world.

Our international responsibilities enrich parish life and deepen genuine Catholic identity. Integrating themes of solidarity into the routines of parish life will make for a richer, more Catholic experience of Church. In giving a little, we receive much more.

All these efforts cannot be cause for complacency. Given the size of our community, our response through the years has not fully reflected our capacity or our calling. While much has been given overall, many of us have given little or nothing. The crisis of solidarity in our world demands more attention, more action, and more generosity from Catholics in the United States.

A Strategy of Integration

We have much to learn from those parishes that are leading the way in making global solidarity an integral part of parish ministry. They understand that

social mission and solidarity are not a task for the few, and that concern for the Church in foreign lands cannot be confined to an occasional small offering. Christ is calling us to do more. In a sense, our parishes need to be more Catholic and less parochial. A suffering world must find a place in the pastoral priorities of every Catholic parish.

Catholic communities of faith should measure their prayer, education, and action by how they serve the life, dignity, and rights of the human person at home *and* abroad. A parish's "catholicity" is illustrated in its willingness to go beyond its own boundaries to extend the Gospel, serve those in need, and work for global justice and peace. This is not a work for a few agencies or one parish committee, but for every believer and every local community of faith. This solidarity is expressed in our prayer and stewardship, how we form our children and invest our resources, and the choices we make at work and in the public arena.

CATHOLIC NEAR EAST WELFARE ASSOCIATION

Catholic Near East Welfare Association (CNEWA) is a special agency of the Holy See established in 1926 to support the pastoral mission and institutions of the Catholic churches of the East and to provide humanitarian assistance to the needy and afflicted without regard to nationality, race, or religion. It also has been entrusted by the Holy Father with the responsibility for promoting the union of the Catholic and Orthodox churches. CNEWA raises and distributes funds to help meet the material and spiritual needs of churches and peoples of the Middle East, Northeast Africa, India, and Eastern Europe and to Eastern Catholics everywhere. Contact:

Catholic Near East Welfare Association
1011 First Avenue
New York, NY 10022
Telephone: (212) 826-1480
Fax: (212) 838-1344
E-mail: bad@cnewa.org

CATHOLIC RELIEF SERVICES
On behalf of the U.S. Catholic community, Catholic Relief Services (CRS) serves millions of poor people all over the world. By responding to victims of disasters, supporting community self-help projects, and contributing to more just societies, CRS provides opportunities for people who have no political voice, no economic power, and no social status. It provides active expression of Christ's love throughout the world and strengthens the local Catholic Church's ability to serve the poor. For American Catholics, CRS is a vehicle to express solidarity with those whom we will never personally meet in more than eighty countries. Contact:

Church Outreach Department
Catholic Relief Services
209 West Fayette Street
Baltimore, MD 21201
Telephone: (410) 625-2220, ext. 3214
Fax: (410) 234-3183
E-mail: wokeefe@catholicrelief.org

These are matters of fundamental justice. Our nation has special responsibilities. Principled and constructive U.S. leadership is essential to build a safer, more just world. As Pope John Paul II insists again and again, our efforts must begin with fundamental reform of the "structures of violence" that bring suffering and death to the poor. The Catholic community will continue to speak on behalf of increased development assistance, relief from international debt, curbs on the arms trade, and respect for human life and the rights of families. We will continue to oppose population policies that insist on inclusion of abortion among the methods of family planning. Our foreign aid and peacemaking efforts can be reformed and improved, but they cannot be abandoned. Massive cuts in recent years in U.S. assistance for the poor around the world are an evasion of our responsibility as a prosperous nation and world leader. The recent decline in resources for sustainable development must be reversed.

It is not only the poor who need our solidarity and advocacy. Our world is still marked by destruction of human life and denial of human rights and religious liberty in so many places. Genuine solidarity requires active and informed citizenship. It requires common action to address the fundamental causes of injustice and the sources of violence in our world.

A "framework for parish global solidarity" is offered at the end of these reflections to help parishes reflect, as communities of faith in a universal Church, on international dimensions of parish life.

Conclusion

The Catholic community in the United States should be proud of the mission, advocacy, humanitarian relief, and development activities of our Church. U.S. Catholics are generous, active, committed, and concerned. But we must recognize that still too many children die, too many weapons are sold, and too many believers are persecuted.

Through the eyes of faith, the starving child, the believer in jail, and the woman without clean water or health care are not issues, but Jesus in disguise. The human and moral costs of the arms trade, international debt, environmental neglect, and ethnic violence are not abstractions, but tests of our faith. Violence in the Holy Land, tribal combat in Africa, religious persecution, and starvation around the world are not just headlines, but a call to action. As Catholics, we are called to renew the earth, not escape its challenge.

Our faith challenges us to reach out to those in need, to take on the global status quo, and to resist the immorality of isolationism. Pope John Paul II reminds us that a turn to "selfish isolation" would not only be a "betrayal of humanity's legitimate expectations . . . but also a real desertion of a moral obligation."

In one sense, we need to move our Church's concern from strong teaching to creative action. Working together, we can continue to help missionaries preach the Gospel, empower poor people in their own development, help the Church live and grow in lands marked by repression and poverty, and assist countries emerging from authoritarian rule. We must help reform and increase development assistance, curb the arms trade, ban landmines, relieve debt, and protect human life and human rights.

Many middle-aged and older Catholics grew up with a keen sense of "mission" and concern for children half a world away. Years ago we raised funds for "pagan babies," cleaned our plates, and prayed after Mass for the conversion of Russia. We didn't have global TV networks or the Internet, but we had a sense of responsibility. Over the years, we have continued this tradition through our missions, our collections for and advocacy on international needs, and our global development programs. We need to acknowledge and renew this traditional Catholic consciousness in a new age of global communications and economic interdependence. We respond very generously when the network news tells us of hurricanes and famines, but how will we help those victimized by the less visible disasters of poverty caused by structural injustice, such as debt, ethnic conflict, and the arms trade? Our Church and parishes must call us anew to sacrifice and concern for a new generation of children who need food, justice, peace, and the Gospel. A central task for the next century is building families of faith that reach out beyond national boundaries.

As we approach the jubilee, let us rediscover in our time the meaning of the mystical body of Christ. We should mark the new millennium by making our families and local communities of faith signs of genuine solidarity—praying, teaching, preaching, and acting with new urgency and creativity on the international obligations of our faith. As our Holy Father has pointed out, "A commitment to justice and peace in a world like ours, marked by so many conflicts and intolerable social and economic inequalities, is a necessary condition for the preparation and celebration of the Jubilee" (*Tertio Millennio Adveniente,* no. 51). This calls us to a new openness, a strategy of integration, and a true commitment to solidarity. In the words of the Apostle Paul, we must strive "to preserve the unity of the spirit through the bond of peace: one body and one Spirit . . . one Lord, one faith, one baptism; one God and Father of all, who is over all and through all and in all" (Eph 4:3-6).

SECRETARIAT FOR LATIN AMERICA

The National Conference of Catholic Bishops' Secretariat for Latin America serves the Committee on the Church in Latin America in responding to the mandate of the U.S. bishops to maintain an active relationship with the Church in Latin America. The secretariat develops and administers the National Collection for the Church in Latin America and manages a program of financial assistance to the Latin American church. An educational program in North America is carried out to inform the U.S. public about the reality of the Church in Latin America and to promote solidarity and a deeper relationship between the Church in the United States and in Latin America. Contact:

Secretariat for Latin America
National Conference of Catholic Bishops
3211 Fourth Street, N.E.
Washington, DC 20017-1194
Telephone: 202-541-3050
Fax: 202-541-3460
E-mail: mtorres-reilly@nccbuscc.org

Appendix:
A Framework for
Parish Global Solidarity

This framework seeks to help parishes explore how to better integrate the international responsibilities of Catholic faith in local communities of faith. It is drawn from *Communities of Salt and Light: Reflections on the Social Mission of the Parish*. The framework is complemented by a parish global solidarity resource, which offers suggestions to parish leaders in assessing and strengthening their parish commitment to global solidarity.

OFFICE TO AID THE CATHOLIC CHURCH IN CENTRAL AND EASTERN EUROPE

The Office to Aid the Catholic Church in Central and Eastern Europe staffs the National Conference of Catholic Bishops' Ad Hoc Committee to Aid the Church in Central and Eastern Europe. The office promotes and administers the U.S. bishops' annual collection for eastern Europe, provides financial support for the Church in central and eastern Europe, and informs U.S. Catholics about the conditions and need of the Church in the post-communist era. The office maintains contact with the Church and the episcopal conferences of eastern Europe and acts as a resource to the bishops in matters regarding the Church of that region. Contact:

Office to Aid the Catholic Church in
Central and Eastern Europe
National Conference of Catholic Bishops
3211 Fourth Street, N.E.
Washington, DC 20017-1194
Telephone: 202-541-3400
Fax: 202-541-3406
E-mail: rgs@nccbuscc.org

Anchoring Solidarity: Prayer, Worship, and Preaching

One of the most important ways to respond to the Catholic call to solidarity is through prayer and worship. In our parishes, the eucharist represents a central setting for discovering and expressing our commitment to our brothers and sisters throughout the world. Gathered around the altar, we are reminded of our connection to all of God's people through the mystical body of Christ. The eucharist makes present the sacrifice of Calvary in which Christ's blood is shed for the redemption of the world. Our call to solidarity has its roots in this mystery and in the Gospel of Jesus Christ, which we proclaim every time we gather for eucharist.

While care must be taken to avoid ideological uses of liturgy, the eucharist and the Gospel call the Church to proclaim and express the global solidarity of the people of God. International concerns can be reflected in the introduction to the Mass, general intercessions, and music. There is no greater opportunity to help Catholics understand the social dimensions of our faith than in the homily. Preachers can connect the gospel message of love for our neighbor and the biblical values of justice and peace to the real struggles of people in other lands that we see on the evening news. Inviting returned missionaries or relief workers to preach or speak to the congregation can provide examples of faith in action that can lead to concrete acts of solidarity. We can also use various collections for missions, development, and relief as opportunities to raise awareness and promote action on the needs of people in other lands. Through prayer, worship, and preaching we can deepen our understanding of the call to build greater justice and peace.

Teaching Solidarity: Education and Formation

Education and formation are key arenas for teaching global solidarity. We strongly support Catholic educators who integrate international concerns into their programs and classes such as geography, history, and science classes, as well as religious education and formation. Many Catholic educators are finding creative ways to reflect and act on the call to global solidarity, from principals and teachers who encourage their students to participate in Lenten relief programs to adult educators who host speakers on missions or international issues.

Solidarity is action on behalf of the one human family, calling us to help overcome the divisions in our world.

While much is being done, too many educational programs still neglect or ignore the global dimensions of our Catholic calling. We urge all Catholic educators to share the Church's teaching on the global dimensions of our social mission more intentionally, more explicitly, and more creatively. We encourage the incorporation of the call to global solidarity into our schools, religious education programs, sacramental preparation, and Christian initiation programs. We need to match efforts to share the principle of solidarity with opportunities to act on it—to share our financial and material resources, to search for the structural causes of poverty, to promote development, and to advocate for human life, human dignity, and human rights.

Living Solidarity: Work, Family, Citizenship

Many choices about international concerns are made in economic and public life. American corporations shape the world as much as government action. Business, union, and government leaders make decisions every day that enhance or undermine human life and dignity around the world. How believers invest and consume—and the choices we make as voters and citizens—can shape a world of greater or lesser justice, more or less peace.

The Church's commitment to global solidarity belongs especially to lay people. It is reflected at least as much in the choices of lay Catholics in commerce and politics as in the statements and advocacy of our bishops' conference. How U.S. businesses act abroad sets standards that advance or diminish justice. Catholics should bring their awareness of global solidarity to their diverse roles in business and commerce, in education and communications, and in the labor movement and public life. As teachers, broadcasters, journalists, and entertainers, Catholics can awaken a sense, not only of the world's problems, but also our capacity to respond. As citizens, we can urge public officials and legislators to seriously address the problems of the world's persecuted, poor, and displaced.

In today's complex world, the demands of solidarity cannot be filled simply by an occasional gift or contribution, although generosity is required of each of us. Solidarity demands responses and initiatives that are as rich and varied as our relationships, responsibilities, and lives.

Investing in Solidarity: Stewardship

Catholics in the United States have given many millions of dollars to reach out to brothers and sisters in other parts of the world. In three decades, Catholics in our country have contributed more than $80 million through our Latin America collection alone. Through the annual collection for the Propagation of the Faith, we support missionaries who share the faith in every part of the world. Through parish collections and other activities, Catholic Relief Services provides not only emergency food to the hungry but also long-term support for development, health care, and sustainable agriculture in 2,000 projects around the world. In our collection for Central and Eastern Europe, Catholics in the United States help to rebuild churches and communities torn apart by years of repression. This is an impressive record of generosity.

One particular example of family stewardship is Operation Rice Bowl of Catholic Relief Services. This Lenten program suggests that families skip a meal or eat only rice. The money saved from these "sacrificial" meals is shared with the poor through CRS. We endorse this and other family signs of solidarity.

While we are proud of and encouraged by the generosity of our people, we know we can do even more. We've seen it so often in our own dioceses.

COMMITTEE ON WORLD MISSION

The National Conference of Catholic Bishops' Committee on World Mission coordinates the U.S. Catholic overseas mission effort, basing itself on the 1986 pastoral statement *To the Ends of the Earth* and subsequent papal encyclicals such as *Redemptoris Missio*. The committee works closely with the Pontifical Missionary Societies, the mission-sending societies of men and women, organizations of lay missioners, and other organizations promoting the mission *ad gentes*, encouraging, supporting, and fostering mission animation efforts in the United States. Contact:

Committee on World Mission
National Conference of Catholic Bishops
3211 Fourth Street, N.E.
Washington, DC 20017-1194
Telephone: 202-541-3411
Fax: 202-541-3322
E-mail: worldmissions@nccbuscc.org

When we see clearly the suffering of others—down the block or half a world away—we respond with remarkable charity and compassion. Our Church calls us to see more clearly the suffering, needs, and potential of our sisters and brothers and helps us respond with even greater generosity and sacrifice.

However, stewardship is about more than how we use our money and resources. All we have comes from God. We are stewards not only of our money, but also our time, our energy, and indeed our whole lives. Stewardship for global solidarity means that we share what we have and what we are to make life better for those who are poor and vulnerable at home and around the world. It means that we take time to work for just policies and a more peaceful world and that we give even more generously to these international collections.

Practicing Solidarity: Outreach and Charity

Parishes are called to help those who suffer in our own communities and in situations of poverty and pain around the world. Turning the human struggle we see on the nightly news into effective parish outreach on a global level demands initiative and creativity. It most often starts with building relationships, sometimes with members of the parish who are from countries where there is war, famine, and human suffering. Or the relationship may begin with our own mission efforts, Catholic Relief Services, or a diocesan resettlement office.

One special way parishes have reached out in solidarity is through a process known as twinning, in which a parish in the United States develops an ongoing relationship with a parish in another part of the world. Our Secretariat for Latin America reports that more than 1,700 parishes in the United States have connected in special relationships with Catholic communities in Central and South America. We welcome "twinning" relationships and encourage the development of these relationships in ways that avoid dependency and paternalism. These bridges of faith offer as much to U.S. parishes as their partners. We are evangelized and changed as we help other communities of faith.

> The Holy Father's call to global responsibility is the core of a Catholic international agenda and the foundation of a Catholic commitment to solidarity.

Promoting Solidarity: Advocacy and Political Responsibility

True parish commitment to global solidarity will not stop with financial aid or compassionate service efforts. Pursuing justice is at the core of the call to solidarity. Parishes can promote a broader, truly universal sense of political responsibility by calling Catholics to be informed and involved in international peace and justice issues, responding to the leadership of the Holy Father. Parishes have special opportunities to develop leadership, to promote citizenship, and to provide forums for discussion and action on global issues. Legislative networks and state Catholic conferences are effective tools for helping believers act on the international dimensions of our faith.

Active citizenship by Catholics is also required if U.S. policies are to reflect our best values and traditions. The voices of parishioners need to be heard on behalf of children who are being destroyed by abortion, starvation, landmines, or lack of health care. We need to be heard as we approach the jubilee on how international debt transfers wealth from poor nations to rich societies and diminishes the lives and integrity of so many. We need to be heard especially on behalf of women, who bear the greatest burdens of poverty and injustice. We need to be heard on behalf of the millions of child laborers in the world. We can insist that U.S. corporations eliminate child laborers in all their assembly operations.

Parishes should offer nonpartisan opportunities for members to register to vote, to become informed on international issues, and to communicate with legislators. We can help convince our nation that building peace, combating poverty and despair, and protecting human life and human rights are not only moral imperatives, but also wise national priorities. We can help shape a world that will be a safer, more secure, and more just home for all of us.

PART II

Suggestions for Action

Introduction

Called to Global Solidarity is a message about action. It calls each individual Catholic and every Catholic parish to a greater sense of commitment to our sisters and brothers around the world. It builds on *Communities of Salt and Light*, the U.S. bishops' statement on the social mission of the parish. It urges us to make real our understanding of the mystical body of Christ through our prayers, through what we teach, and through concrete actions to serve the needs of the poor and to work for greater justice in international policies.

This challenge can seem overwhelming. The many demands and pressures on our families and parish volunteers—as well as the complexity of international issues—can make it difficult to figure out how to really make a difference.

But it doesn't have to be difficult. Individual Catholics and parishes all over our country are finding creative ways to act on the international dimensions of our faith. These efforts range from things as simple as participating in our collections for international assistance and missions, to international parish twinning relationships, to sending medical missions into foreign lands. For individuals and parishes involved in international activities, these efforts are enriching and transforming.

The following suggestions for action are drawn from these varied experiences. They offer ideas for parishes, following the framework outlined in the bishops' statement on the social mission of the parish, *Communities of Salt and Light*. They are intended to spark creativity and to be adapted to the unique context and resources of each individual and parish.

The parish's call to global solidarity is not a project or program that can be completed in a month, a year, or even a decade. It is an ongoing journey, a way of life that consistently reflects our love and concern for all our sisters and brothers, wherever they might live. The best parish strategies for acting on this call begin at the center of the parish's life and are integrated throughout its ministries. The following suggestions reflect this strategy of integration.

How to Get Started

An important starting point for parish efforts to act on the global dimensions of our faith is careful planning by the pastor and parish leadership. You may want to use a staff meeting and/or a parish council meeting to consider how to renew or strengthen your parish's commitment to global solidarity.

- Begin by viewing the video, *Global Solidarity*, or by reading the statement's section on "Theological Foundations" and using the discussion questions on page 25. This can help the group gain a common understanding of the roots of our commitment to international peace and justice. The *Catechism of the Catholic Church* also includes many passages that highlight our call to global solidarity (see especially nos. 1939-1942).

- Assess your parish's current efforts to contribute to global solidarity. The questions on pages 14-15 are designed to help you assess what your parish is already doing and where it might strengthen its efforts.

- Consider how international concerns might be better integrated into your parish's ministries and programs. You may want to copy and distribute to appropriate staff and volunteers the suggestions for various parish ministries that begin on page 15.

- Contact your diocesan offices for missions, social action, and Catholic Relief Services to get their advice and to find out about international programs that are sponsored by the diocese.

Called to Global Solidarity is a message about action. It calls each individual Catholic and every Catholic parish to a greater sense of commitment to our sisters and brothers around the world.

- Develop a written plan listing the specific steps you will take, identifying who is responsible, and outlining your timeframe. One starting point might be copying and distributing at Masses and other parish gatherings the "Suggestions for Individuals and Families" handout on page 26.

- Identify leaders who will carry out your plan. Your parish social concerns or social justice committee can play a leadership role in helping to coordinate parish efforts to address the international demands of our faith. If you don't already have such a committee, contact your diocesan social action director for help with strategies for creating one.

Remember as you move forward that there is no "right" way to act on the message in *Called to Global*

**REFUGEE SPONSORSHIP
ST. TERESA OF AVILA PARISH,
PERRYSVILLE, PENN.**

St. Teresa of Avila parish was approached by Catholic Charities of the Diocese of Pittsburgh to help resettle a Bosnian refugee family from the war-ravaged Balkans region. Once the pastor of St. Teresa heard of the appeal, he asked the parish's social minister, Sr. Irene Moeller, OSB, to see what could be done to help the family.

Through the efforts of individual volunteers, as well as parish organizations such as the St. Vincent de Paul Society, the Ladies' Guild, and Christian Mothers, and the parish council, Sr. Irene was able to organize parish sponsorship of the family for one year. The parish established a fund-raising effort which included a second collection and ongoing appeals for donations to support the resettlement effort. Parish volunteers were organized into groups to conduct various tasks associated with the resettlement, such as furnishing the household, transportation, and education. The St. Teresa volunteers have befriended the refugee family and have welcomed them into their community.

Solidarity. Each parish is a unique community whose members have special gifts, talents, and experiences. Your next step, whether a modest effort or a major project, will work best if it reflects the particular needs and opportunities of your community of faith. The following suggestions may help trigger your own ideas and plans.

Assessment Questions

1. *General.* Where does the call to global solidarity fit into the life of our parish? Is it a central and consistent commitment for our entire community of faith or a task left to a few committee members or individuals?

   - Do parishioners understand what solidarity means? Has our parish helped them think about what it would mean to be in solidarity around the world?

   - What do we know about our parish's connection to international issues? Are there parishioners from different parts of the world who could be helpful in sharing their experiences, developing a special project, or establishing a twinning relationship with another parish? Is there an immigrant or refugee community in the area with which our parish could connect? Do our parishioners have particular skills or resources that they would like to share?

   - Have we contacted our diocesan offices for missions, social action, and/or Catholic Relief Services to find out about international projects sponsored by the diocese?

2. *Anchoring Solidarity: Prayer, Worship, and Preaching.* How is our concern for our sisters and brothers around the world reflected in our parish's prayer, worship, and preaching? Is this theme appropriately and regularly woven into the homilies? Is it reflected in general intercessions, special prayer services, and the prayers that open parish meetings?

3. *Teaching Solidarity: Education and Formation.* How is our Church's teaching on international justice and peace taught in our parish's education programs? Do we hold adult education programs on church teaching and/or international policy issues? Do our religious education and sacramental preparation programs include

**MISSION PARTNERSHIP
DIOCESE OF JOLIET, ILL.**

After exploring several possible sites for medical mission work in Bolivia, and upon the invitation of Archbishop Jesús Perez Rodriguez, the Diocese of Joliet began a mission partnership with the Archdiocese of Sucre, Bolivia in 1993. Teams of U.S. doctors and nurses worked side-by-side with Bolivian doctors, performing specialty surgeries and treatments at no cost for some of Sucre's poorest residents. The U.S. teams taught surgical and follow-up procedures, enabling the Bolivians to continue to care for these and future patients.

Learning that many of the illnesses treated by the medical teams were related to living conditions, the Diocese of Joliet formed a Catholic Construction Corps. Teams are now sent periodically to help upgrade homes in the barrios to aid in the prevention of certain diseases. The mission partnership also includes cooperation from the religious education and the youth ministry groups of the diocese. A "Sister Diocese Commission" has been formed in Sucre with a part-time staff paid by the Diocese of Joliet.

opportunities to study and act on church teaching on global solidarity? If we have a parish school, are students taught about the Church's teaching on peace and justice? Are they given opportunities to act on this teaching?

4. *Living Solidarity: Work, Family, and Citizenship.* How does our parish encourage individuals and families to reflect a commitment to international justice and peace in their family, work, and public lives? Are they given information about the impact of their consumer choices on workers around the world? Do we acknowledge and affirm those who work in the area of international concerns (e.g., missionary programs, foreign service, or Peace Corps)? Are parishioners encouraged to participate in political life in ways that promote international justice and peace?

5. *Investing in Solidarity: Stewardship.* How are collections for Catholic international programs handled? Are they seriously explained and promoted? Do preachers link the Gospel to these collections? Are they seen as opportunities to share Catholic teaching on international concerns?

6. *Practicing Solidarity: Outreach and Charity.* How does our parish respond to the urgent needs of people around the world? Are parishioners given opportunities to share their financial resources with those who live in poverty in other lands? Do we participate in programs that allow parishioners with particular skills (e.g., medical personnel or carpenters) to share their talents?

7. *Promoting Solidarity: Advocacy and Political Responsibility.* What information and opportunities are given to parishioners regarding international peace and justice issues? Does our parish participate in a legislative network? Are "action alerts" on international issues shared through the bulletin or through a telephone tree or mailing list?

Whether you identified a few or many opportunities for strengthening your parish's commitment to global solidarity, the key is to identify some realistic and achievable next steps. The following suggestions are designed to help you in this planning process.

Anchoring Solidarity: Prayer, Worship, and Preaching

- Make a commitment that parish activities—staff meetings, parish council meetings, other activities—will be started with a prayer for global solidarity in general or for a particular intention that has international dimensions.

- Identify feast days, collections, and other events during the year when a focus on global solidarity would be appropriate during liturgies and other activities. During liturgical seasons such as Lent and Advent, our focus on giving and doing "good works" can lead us to a greater commitment to our sisters and brothers in need around the world. The "Global Solidarity Calendar" on page 28 can help you identify some of these events.

- During Sunday and daily liturgies, incorporate concern for the poor, refugees, and victims of war

**CAMPAIGN TO BAN LANDMINES
ST. PAUL'S PARISH, SEATTLE, WASH.**

St. Paul's parish in Seattle chose a Sunday in October 1997 for a special focus on the Catholic Campaign to Ban Landmines. In preparation, the school's eighth-grade teacher worked with her students to study and produce materials for the parish. A visiting homilist showed *Killing Fields*, a video on the landmines crisis, for his homily. Various educational materials were distributed after Masses. More than 400 people signed appeals to the president and members of Congress urging them to work for a ban on landmines.

---

and disasters around the world in the introductory comments, the general intercessions, and the homilies. The "Global Solidarity Calendar" on page 28 can identify days when these themes are particularly appropriate. For example, on Pentecost Sunday, parts of the Mass can be spoken in different languages by parishioners who have lived in other countries. Your choice of music can also reflect a focus on global solidarity.

- Use liturgical materials provided for special collections and other events (e.g., American Bishops' Overseas Appeal, Collection for the Church in Latin America, Aid to the Church in Central and Eastern Europe, World Mission Sunday, National Migration Week).
- Offer a special Mass welcoming refugees and others who have come to your community from foreign lands. A special Mass might also be offered for those who are going to serve overseas through international missionary, relief, and service organizations.

- Learn about the special feasts and religious traditions of the ethnic communities in your area and celebrate them as a parish. If you are twinned with a parish in a foreign country, use the special feasts of the twinned community, including the parish's patron saint, as opportunities to raise awareness. Information on "twinning" or "sister parish" programs can be found on page 21.

- Ask prayer groups and other small faith sharing groups in the parish to regularly focus on the Church's call to global solidarity.

- During Lent, participate in Operation Rice Bowl, a Lenten program of prayer, fasting, learning, and giving sponsored by Catholic Relief Services. Free materials are available from CRS that offer suggestions for parishes, teachers, and families to integrate global concerns into their prayer and faith lives. See the Operation Rice Bowl description on page 18.

- When appropriate, make connections in homilies between lectionary readings about how we treat "widows, orphans, and aliens" and the "least among us," as well as those about the "mystical body of Christ" and other themes to the present-day needs of our sisters and brothers around the world.

- Use information from the fact sheet on page 29 in homilies to illustrate the current needs of our "neighbors" around the globe.

- Use other resources to develop homilies focused on international concerns. Catholic Relief Services has produced a booklet, *Preaching the Global Gospel*, that offers global reflections for homilists. The USCC Secretariat for Latin America publishes *Una Vista*, a biannual newsletter mailed to all parishes which contains information about the Church in Latin America. Helpful materials are also produced in connection with most of the international collections and events (American Bishops' Overseas Appeal, Collection for the Church in Latin America, Aid to the Church in Central and Eastern Europe, World Mission Sunday, National Migration Week). These and other suggestions for homilists can be found in the resource listing on pages 32-40.

- Invite returned missionaries to give a homily and/or speak at the end of Mass about their experiences in other lands. To identify potential speakers, contact your diocesan director for the Propagation of the Faith.

Teaching Solidarity: Education and Formation

Adult Education

- Consider sponsoring special adult programs on global solidarity as well as incorporating this theme into the meetings of ongoing groups (e.g., women's or men's groups, senior citizens' groups).

- Ask an adult education class or another parish group to read and discuss *Called to Global Solidarity* and/or materials produced by Catholic Relief Services, United States Catholic Conference (USCC) Migration and Refugee Services, the USCC Secretariat for Latin America, and other Catholic groups that focus on international concerns. (See the resource listing beginning on page 32 and the discussion questions on page 25.)

OPPOSING SWEATSHOPS
DIOCESE OF SCRANTON, PENN.

The Social Concerns Office of the Diocese of Scranton assisted in a community effort to deepen public awareness of sweatshops, child labor, and other labor abuses. Their participation was part of the National Labor Committee's "Day of Conscience/Holiday Season of Conscience" to end child labor and sweatshop abuse.

The local activities included an ecumenical prayer service which involved people from various faith communities, labor unions, and community organizations. Following the service some participants went to local shopping areas to pass out pamphlets as part of a public education campaign.

These events were intended to strengthen solidarity with victims worldwide who are being exploited in the workplace. The events have made consumers and participants in the local marketplace more sensitive to the issues of social justice.

- Watch the video, *Global Solidarity*, which provides a thought-provoking summary of the bishops' message on global solidarity. The questions on page 25 can be used to structure a follow-up discussion.

- Use the bulletin quotes on pages 30-31 to share the basic message of *Called to Global Solidarity.*

- Copy and distribute at Masses and other parish gatherings the "Suggestions for Individuals and Families" handout on pages 26-27.

- Invite a recent immigrant, a returned missionary, a former Peace Corps volunteer, a Catholic Relief Services staff person on home leave, or a pastor or leader from your "sister parish" to describe the conditions and needs in other parts of the world. Contact your diocesan resettlement director, ethnic ministries director, Propagation of the Faith director, or Catholic Relief Services director to identify potential speakers. More information on "twinning" or "sister parish" relationships can be found on page 21.

- Use National Migration Week, held in January each year, as an opportunity to teach about the needs of immigrants and refugees. For information about obtaining a complete parish implementation kit, contact your diocesan migration and refugee office or USCC Migration and Refugee Services (202-541-3352).

- Include in your adult education sessions opportunities for participants to act; our call to global solidarity is not just a call to greater understanding, but a call to action. (See the suggestions for "outreach and charity" and "advocacy" beginning on page 21.)

- Participate in Catholic Relief Service's (CRS) Operation Rice Bowl—a Lenten program of prayer, fasting, learning, and giving. Operation Rice Bowl offers helpful educational materials for parishes and families. Contact your diocesan CRS director for information.

- Participate in "Frontiers of Justice," a program sponsored by Catholic Relief Services that gives Catholic secondary school teachers an opportunity to learn about issues of international development and global justice by visiting a CRS project overseas. For information, contact Catholic Relief Services Church Outreach Office (800-235-2772).

**SMALL GRANTS PROGRAM
DIOCESE OF SAGINAW, MICH.**

The Office of Christian Service of the Diocese of Saginaw has developed a small grants program to support parishes involved in international concerns and global solidarity. The funds come from the diocesan share of the proceeds from Operation Rice Bowl. Parishes have used the grants to hold film festivals, sell crafts from developing countries, bring in speakers, attend educational programs, and organize simulation games on hunger and power. The Office of Christian Service also has a fund for lay people to visit Catholic Relief Service sites and other programs in developing countries.

Schools, Religious Education Programs, and Youth Groups

- Sponsor a child in a developing country, involving the students in raising the necessary money and sharing information on conditions in the sponsored child's country. See the child sponsorship programs listed on page 22.

- Ask students to do research on another country and/or an area of crisis, or ask them to clip newspaper and magazine stories. They can also be asked to research where their clothing comes from and the working conditions of those who make their clothing. Discuss the conditions and issues they identify in the context of Catholic teaching on peace and justice.

- Encourage students and/or related groups (e.g., scouting groups) to develop pen pal relationships with children in a "sister parish." This project can be expanded to include Christmas boxes and school supply boxes. See the information on establishing a "sister parish" or "twinning relationship" on page 21.

- Integrate Catholic teaching about global solidarity into sacramental preparation programs. For example, children preparing for first eucharist can begin to understand how the eucharist connects us to all of our sisters and brothers, wherever they might live. The sacraments of baptism and confirmation and the Rite of Christian Initiation also offer important opportunities to share this message.

- Sponsor a poster or essay contest on a topic related to global solidarity. Posters can be displayed in church vestibules and other visible spots to focus broader attention on the topic.

- Use *Who Are My Sisters and Brothers?*, an educational project designed to help children and adults understand and welcome immigrants and refugees. It offers background materials for educators, lesson plans, handouts, outlines for retreats, and prayer services. A twenty-seven-minute video with a discussion guide is also available. The project was cosponsored by USCC Migration and Refugee Services, the National Catholic Educational Association, the National Conference for Catechetical Leadership, the National Conference for Interracial Justice, and the National Federation for Catholic Youth Ministry. For information, contact Migration and Refugee Services (202-541-3230).

- Display the posters produced for most of the international collections and events (e.g., American Bishops' Overseas Appeal, Collection for the Church in Latin America, Aid to the Church in Central and Eastern Europe, Operation Rice Bowl, National Migration Week) in visible spots where they can help strengthen awareness of our call to global solidarity.

- Invite recent immigrants, returned missionaries, former Peace Corps volunteers, or others with overseas experience to speak to your school or class.

- Participate in one or more of Catholic Relief Services' educational programs, which have complete, easy-to-use materials. For information on these programs, contact CRS (800-235-2772).

Operation Rice Bowl is a Lenten program that calls Catholics in the United States to pray, fast, learn, and give to those in need around the world. It provides a spiritual experience of Lent focused on the poor overseas. It teaches the values of self-sacrifice and concern for the poor. Parishes and schools receive free materials to distribute to families during Lent.

Work of Human Hands, which is cosponsored with SERRV International, helps schools and parishes educate about global economic issues by incorporating the crafts of people from more than forty countries into school or parish bazaars, fairs, holiday festivals, and other events. Eighty percent of the money raised is used to support the artisans and cover low administrative costs. The remaining 20 percent is split between the sponsoring group and the diocese. A kit is available with suggestions for integrating the program into the curriculum and programs of the school.

**SUPPORT FOR MISSION IN BRAZIL
ST. RAPHAEL PARISH, SPRINGFIELD, OHIO**

The social justice and peace committee of St. Raphael Parish in Springfield responded to news of the murder of a priest working for social justice in Brazil by studying conditions in Brazil and contacting their member of Congress about U.S. policy toward Brazil. After further prayer and reflection, the committee decided to develop a missionary relationship with the people of Brazil. The committee obtained a list of missionaries working in Brazil from their archdiocesan mission office and sent letters to five missionaries requesting information about their work. After receiving responses from the missionaries, the committee decided to support the ministry of Sr. Dorothy Stang in Centro Nazare. Two representatives from the archdiocesan mission office came to talk to the committee about the nature of a parish twinning relationship.

The parishioners of St. Raphael sent funds to help Sr. Dorothy build a much-needed community center for the people's spiritual and social development needs. Through a visit by parish representatives to Centro Nazare and a visit to St. Raphael by Sr. Dorothy, the parish deepened its relationship with the people at Centro Nazare and learned about their culture, social conditions, and deep faith.

Food Fast is a twenty-four-hour hunger awareness program designed to engage youth in grades 8 through 12 in addressing the needs of their sisters and brothers around the world. The program includes prayer, reflection, and activities that demonstrate the reality of severe inequalities in meeting basic human needs.

- Consider participating in the Holy Childhood Association (HCA) intercultural educational program and using their materials for seasonal appeals at Halloween, Advent, and Lent. Parishes and schools can distribute offering boxes to help less fortunate children in more than one hundred countries. Contact HCA (202-775-8637) for more information.

- Consider using two resources from the Columban Fathers: "Come and See" for children in grades K through 6, and "Challenged and Empowered" for children in middle and high school. Both programs include videos, lesson plans, and other written materials for focusing on the theme of mission and such issues as world poverty and hunger. Contact the Columban Fathers (402-291-1920) for more information.

Living Solidarity: Work, Family, and Citizenship

- Through homilies, bulletin reminders, and your religious education programs, encourage families to regularly include in their prayers those who are suffering around the world.

- On appropriate feast days and other parish events that focus on global solidarity, acknowledge and affirm the individuals and families in your parish who have come from, or who have served in, other lands.

- Help parents teach their children how their choices affect people around the world. For example, bulletins, adult education sessions, and school newsletters can encourage families to avoid investing in and purchasing goods from companies that exploit workers, especially children. For information on organizations that oppose sweatshops, contact the USCC Department of Social Development and World Peace (202-541-3180).

- Encourage parishioners to substitute for their vacation a stay at a Catholic mission in a developing country. For information about opportunities for families, contact Maryknoll's "Call and Response" program (10636 North 37th Avenue, Phoenix, AZ 85029).

- Encourage individuals to join international volunteer programs. The Catholic Network of Volunteer Service (800-543-5046) annually publishes a list of Catholic volunteer opportunities.

- Use bulletin inserts and special adult education sessions before national elections to offer voter education on Catholic social teaching and its application to international issues. Encourage parishioners to participate in legislative advocacy and to consider these issues as they cast their votes.

- Research the international activities of local corporations. Do they maintain codes of conduct in the areas of working conditions, safety, and child labor?

Investing in Solidarity: Stewardship

- Make the most of the Church's international collections, which are excellent opportunities for individuals and families to use their resources to serve those in need around the world and to promote economic development and global peace. The primary international collections are listed below. Promotion kits are available for each collection. Contact your diocesan social action, Catholic Relief Services, or missions office for more information.

American Bishops' Overseas Appeal (ABOA). Generally held during Lent each year, ABOA gives Catholics in the United States an opportunity to contribute to programs for international emergency relief and development, assistance to victims of natural disasters, aid to immigrants and refugees, and advocacy on behalf of the poor and vulnerable around the world.

Collection for the Church in Latin America. Generally held each January, the bishops' Collection for the Church in Latin America is an opportunity to assist the Church in Latin America and to support educational programs that promote greater solidarity between the Catholic communities in the United States and in Latin America.

SISTER PARISH PROJECT
ST. CHARLES BORROMEO PARISH, ARLINGTON, VA.

St. Charles Borromeo parish in Arlington has maintained a twinning relationship with two parishes in southwest Haiti (Cavaillon and Gros Marin) for the past ten years. The pastors make annual visits, and parishioners from St. Charles have visited their sister parishes and provided development assistance in four areas:

Economic Development. St. Charles contributed seed money for a small loan program as well as support for women's microenterprise loans.

Educational Development. St. Charles contributed funding for the construction of a high school and for classroom materials in Cavaillon, and worked with a neighboring parish in Arlington to erect an elementary school in Gros Marin.

Church Development. St. Charles tithes 10 percent of its weekly collection to various groups. Once a month the tithe goes to both parishes in Haiti for basic operational support, including stipends for lay leaders and catechists, and education and training for teachers.

Health Care. St. Charles has provided funds for the renovation of an old health care clinic and plans to construct a new building for the clinic in the near future.

In addition to the monthly tithe, the St. Charles Haiti Committee raises funds for specific needs, often through the sale of Haitian crafts.

Aid for the Church in Central and Eastern Europe. Generally held each year on Ash Wednesday, the bishops' Aid for the Church in Central and Eastern Europe is an opportunity to provide financial support for the Church in central and eastern Europe and to support efforts to inform Catholics in the

United States about the conditions and needs of the Church in the post-communist era.

World Mission Sunday. Generally held each year on the next to the last Sunday of October, the World Mission Sunday collection is an opportunity to support the Church's worldwide missionary work by offering prayer and financial support for the Propagation of the Faith.

- Offer opportunities for families to make economic choices that promote global solidarity. For example, during Advent you can sponsor an alternative gift fair through CRS's "Work of Human Hands Program"; during Lent you can promote CRS's Operation Rice Bowl, which encourages families to contribute toward international hunger relief. Both programs are described on page18.

- Invest money in ways that promote international justice and peace. Catholic Relief Services has developed the DEVCAP (Development Capital) Shared Return Fund, a socially responsible, no-load mutual fund that provides investors the opportunity to automatically share a portion of their returns with small business development efforts around the world. (For information, call 800-235-2772.) Other responsible investment assistance services for institutions are also available. For information, contact the USCC Department of Social Development and World Peace (202-541-3189).

- Consider contributing a portion of your parish's income to international development and relief programs.

Practicing Solidarity: Outreach and Charity

- Consider entering into a "twinning" or "sister parish" relationship. This involves building an ongoing relationship between your parish and a parish in a developing country. The best twinning relationships involve the whole parish and are mutually helpful.

Prayers for the "sister parish" are included in Masses at both the U.S. parish and the overseas parish. School and religious education students from both parishes exchange letters. Regular correspondence from both pastors is printed in the bulletins or read after Mass. The pastor or leaders from the sister parish may visit the U.S. parish, speaking at all the Masses, attending special meetings and receptions, and generally educating U.S. parishioners about their country. Sometimes groups from the U.S. parish visit their sister parish to help with a construction program, to provide medical or dental service, or to assist with another special project.

U.S. parishes usually provide financial and material resources through a collection of money as well as collections of clothes, school supplies, food, and other items. For information on opportunities to develop twinning relationships, contact the USCC Office of International Justice and Peace (202-541-3199).

- Respond to the needs of those in crisis—and to the needs of our own people to help the desperate situations they see on the news—by collecting funds for relief and assistance. Contact your diocesan director for Catholic Relief Services for advice.

- Learn about the unique needs of different regions of the world. For information on opportunities to serve those in Eastern Europe, contact the U.S. Catholic bishops' Office to Aid the Church in Central and Eastern Europe (202-541-3400). For information on opportunities to serve those in Latin America, contact the U.S. Catholic bishops' Secretariat for Latin America (202-541-3050).

HOME CONSTRUCTION IN MEXICO
ST. CYRIL AND OUR MOTHER OF SORROWS PARISHES, TUCSON, ARIZ.

St. Cyril and Our Mother of Sorrows parishes in Tucson are working with Habitat for Humanity to organize bimonthly trips across the border to the *colonias* of Nogales, Sonora, Mexico. Parishioners join with families in the *colonias* to build cinder block homes. Other parishes in the area are supporting the efforts of a program called "First Nation." They collect stuffed toys, which are picked up at the border by indigenous women from northern Mexico who refurbish the toys and distribute them to children in impoverished communities.

**CRS/HARVEST OF HOPE
DIOCESE OF SPOKANE, WASH.**

Cash and wheat valued at over $32,000 were sent to the Diocese of Cochabamba, Bolivia, through "Catholic Relief Services/Harvest of Hope," a joint project of the Diocese of Spokane and Catholic Relief Services (CRS). The wheat was distributed on a food-for-work project in four poor Bolivian communities in the mountainous subtropical area of Tiraque. The communities are participating in the CRS self-help program with training in improved techniques for crop production, irrigation systems, conservation, and reforestation. According to Jose Maguina, the CRS country representative in Bolivia, the project will have an impact beyond material assistance. "The farmers in Cochabamba will realize that they are not alone and that they have brothers and sisters who care about them and want to help them improve their situation." In November 1997, Bishop William S. Skylstad led a delegation of people from the Spokane diocese to Bolivia to learn about CRS projects in that country.

- Sponsor a refugee family or collect household items for a family being resettled. Contact your diocesan office for Migration and Refugee Services or Catholic Charities for more information.

- Sponsor a needy child. The Catholic Near East Welfare Association, a papal agency for humanitarian and pastoral support, offers opportunities to sponsor children in Ethiopia, India, Jordan, Lebanon, and other parts of the Middle East (212-826-1480). "Help-a-Child," cosponsored by the National Council of Catholic Women and Catholic Relief Services, offers opportunities to sponsor children in India, Thailand, Brazil, and Africa (202-682-0334).

- Support the installation of clean water supply facilities in developing communities through "Water for Life," a program sponsored by the National Council of Catholic Women (NCCW) and Catholic Relief Services. For more information, contact NCCW (202-682-0334).

- Work with your diocesan social action or missions office and/or local interfaith groups on such efforts as the CROPWALK, sending medical mission teams to developing areas, and emergency collections.

Promoting Solidarity: Advocacy and Political Responsibility

- Identify where you will get information on international policy issues. Contact your diocesan social action office to learn about resources and information they offer. The USCC Department of Social Development and World Peace (202-541-3180) provides information on international policy issues, including background information and "action alerts" identifying important times to contact government leaders. The Internet can also be a source of information. A list of other sources of information on international policy can be found beginning on page 32.

- Share information on international policy issues with members of your parish. Such issues as relieving Third World debt, promoting humanitarian assistance and development, and banning antipersonnel landmines have important moral dimensions that need to be considered in the Catholic community. The U.S. bishops' statement on political responsibility and mailings from the USCC Department of Social Development and World Peace (202-541-3191) are useful sources for this information. You may want to consider regularly including in your bulletin information on international policy issues and how Catholic social teaching has been applied to them, and sponsoring periodic adult education sessions on international issues. You may also want to invite representatives from the diocesan social action office, local Pax Christi affiliates, or other appropriate groups.

- Provide easy opportunities for your parishioners to act on public policy issues. Often, international issues seem very complex and it is difficult for individuals to figure out what they can do. Forming a legislative network and receiving "action alerts" from organizations that follow international policy regularly is one way to make participation easy. If your parish is not already a part of a diocesan legislative network, contact your diocesan social action office to determine if such a network exists. If so, they can help you form a chapter in your parish. If not, consider forming a legislative advocacy group in the parish that receives information on international policy issues directly from national church organizations. The USCC Department of Social Development and World Peace has a workbook explaining the details of setting up a legislative network (202-541-3195).

- Organize a postcard or letter-writing campaign on specific international policy issues. You can develop a campaign yourself or work with your diocese or other local and national groups. Bread for the World (202-269-0200) is one group that provides kits for these campaigns.

- Organize a meeting on international policy issues between members of your parish and your representatives in the U.S. House and/or Senate when they are in town. If a meeting with a member of Congress is not possible, a meeting with their local staff can be very productive in communicating information on a specific issue and in building a relationship that will strengthen your advocacy in the future.

- Conduct a nonpartisan voter registration drive after Mass or during parish events.

- Prior to elections, sponsor a nonpartisan candidates' forum. This can be done in conjunction with other Catholic parishes or with an interfaith group. The USCC Department of Social Development and World Peace (202-541-3191) offers "do's" and "don'ts" for structuring a forum.

Conclusion

For some individuals and parishes, these suggestions for action will reflect many activities already integrated into their lives and programs. For others, the list may seem overwhelming. The message of *Called to Global Solidarity* is a message for the already engaged, the newly committed, and everyone in between. It says to each of us that no matter how much or how little we're already doing, we can do more. Every step that we take, from the most modest to the most elaborate, is an important response to a central demand of the Gospel of Jesus Christ. We *are* our brothers' and sisters' keepers. *Called to Global Solidarity* asks each individual and every parish to take new steps to strengthen and deepen our understanding of what global solidarity means, to respond to those in need, and to work for global peace and justice. We hope these suggestions for action will

**OPERATION RICE BOWL IN ACTION
ST. MARY'S PARISH, BUFFALO GROVE, ILL.**

Parishioners at St. Mary's are working to build global solidarity through Operation Rice Bowl (ORB), Catholic Relief Services' Lenten program of prayer, fasting, learning, and giving. They start with Ash Wednesday, when rice bowls and family home guides are distributed at the liturgy. They continue to focus on ORB in the liturgies throughout Lent through the prayers of the faithful and the homilies. They encourage the use of the family home guide, which has stories and recipes from countries where Catholic Relief Services is actively helping people to help themselves. St. Mary's also ensures that ORB is integrated into the curriculum of its parish school and religious education program.

One of the most popular Lenten activities at St. Mary's is the "Global Hunger Dinner." Ten percent of the participants receive a meal that is typical of the western world, 20 percent receive a soup and bread meal to represent less developed nations, and 70 percent receive a simple meal of rice to represent the developing world. These percentages are roughly equal to the typical distribution of food and resources in the world. Through prayer and theological reflection, people at the dinner enrich their solidarity with the poor in the developing world and explore how we are all one human family.

stimulate the creativity of the Catholic community as we respond to this important challenge.

[Our] social mission and solidarity are not tasks for the few. . . . Concern for the Church in foreign lands cannot be confined to just an occasional small offering. Christ calls us to do more. In a sense, our parishes need to be more Catholic and less parochial. A suffering world must find a place in the pastoral priorities of every Catholic parish.

PART III

Handouts and Resources

Called to **GLOBAL SOLIDARI†Y** _____ **Discussion Questions**

1. The roots of our call to global solidarity can be found in the Scriptures and the teaching of our Church. How would you describe these "roots"?

2. In your daily life, how are you already responding to the call to global solidarity? In what ways are you ignoring the call or even contributing to global injustices?

3. How is your parish already responding to the call to global solidarity?

4. The bishops' statement on global solidarity encourages Catholics in the United States to work for "fundamental reform of the 'structures of violence' which bring suffering and death to the poor." What do you think they mean by this?

5. The bishops encourage Catholics in the United States to respond to the basic needs of the poor around the world and to work on such issues as human rights, economic development, arms trade, international debt, and environmental neglect. What are the moral dimensions of this challenge? How might you respond?

6. The bishops' statement offers a framework and suggestions for individuals and parishes to promote global solidarity. Which suggestions struck you as ideas you or your parish might be able to adopt?

SUGGESTIONS FOR INDIVIDUALS AND FAMILIES

In November 1997, the Catholic bishops of the United States issued *Called to Global Solidarity*, a statement urging the Catholic community in the United States to strengthen its efforts to reach out to our sisters and brothers in need around the world.

The call to global solidarity is not just a challenge for every diocese and parish, but an obligation of each individual Catholic. As the bishops point out:

> We have heard the Lord's command, "Love your neighbor as yourself." In our linked and limited world, loving our neighbor has global implications. In faith, we know our neighbors live in Rwanda and Sudan, in East Timor and China, in Bosnia and Central America, as well as across our country and next door. . . . Continuing participation in the body of Christ calls us to action for the "least among us" without regard for boundaries or borders.

The following suggestions, which are based on the framework outlined in the appendix to *Called to Global Solidarity*, are designed to help individuals and families identify ways they can more fully respond to this challenge.

Anchoring Solidarity: Prayer and Worship

- Make a commitment to pray regularly for international justice and peace. Keep those in need around the world, as well as those in positions to make important international decisions, in your prayers.

Teaching Solidarity: Education and Formation

- Follow stories about international issues in the news and consider how these issues relate to Catholic social teaching. Encourage your children to do the same, and include these issues in family discussions at the dinner table and elsewhere.

- Read statements from the Holy Father and the U.S. bishops on international policy issues. For information, contact the USCC Department of Social Development and World Peace (202-541-3199).

- Attend meetings, lectures, and other events at your parish or in your community that focus on international concerns.

Living Solidarity: Work, Family, and Citizenship

- Teach your children how their choices affect people around the world. Avoid investing in and purchasing goods from companies that exploit workers, especially children. For information on organizations that oppose sweatshops, contact the USCC Department of Social Development and World Peace (202-541-3180).

- Before voting, consider how Catholic social teaching on international peace and justice might affect your decision.

- Use your vacation time to spend a week or two at a Catholic mission in a developing country. For information about opportunities for families, contact Maryknoll's "Call and Response" program (10636 North 37th

Avenue, Phoenix, AZ 85029). Opportunities for individuals to join international volunteer programs can be obtained from the Catholic Network of Volunteer Service (800-543-5046).

Investing in Solidarity: Stewardship

- Share your resources by generously participating in the Church's collections for international aid and development.

- In both your work and personal life, make efforts to invest in and purchase from companies that do not exploit workers or natural resources and companies that promote international justice and peace. Catholic Relief Services has developed the DEVCAP (Development Capital) Shared Return Fund, a socially responsible, no-load mutual fund that provides investors the opportunity to automatically share a portion of their returns with small business development efforts around the world (800-235-2772).

Practicing Solidarity: Outreach and Charity

- If your parish or another organization holds a collection of food, clothing, or other materials for those in need around the world, offer goods as well as your time to help coordinate it.

- Participate in your parish's "twinning" or "sister parish" program. If your parish doesn't have a twinning relationship with a parish overseas, take the lead in starting one. For information on twinning opportunities, contact your diocesan director for social action or the USCC Office for International Justice and Peace (202-541-3199).

- "Adopt" a refugee family or collect household items for a family being resettled. Contact your diocesan office for Migration and Refugee Services or Catholic Charities for more information.

- Sponsor a needy child. The Catholic Near East Welfare Association, a papal agency for humanitarian and pastoral support, offers opportunities to sponsor children in Ethiopia, India, Jordan, Lebanon, and other parts of the Middle East (212-826-1480). "Help-a-Child," cosponsored by the National Council of Catholic Women and Catholic Relief Services, offers opportunities to sponsor children in India, Thailand, Brazil, and Africa (202-682-0334).

Promoting Solidarity: Advocacy and Political Responsibility

- Join a parish or diocesan legislative network and participate in letter-writing and telephone campaigns on international peace and justice issues. If your parish or diocese doesn't have a legislative network, consider taking the lead in starting one. For information on starting a legislative network in your parish and/or to individually obtain information on international policy issues, contact your diocesan social action office.

The message of *Called to Global Solidarity* is a message for each of us. It challenges us, no matter how much or how little we are doing already, to find a way to strengthen our commitment to global solidarity. It reminds us that every effort that we make, from the most modest to the most elaborate, is an important response to a central demand of the Gospel of Jesus Christ.

Called to GLOBAL SOLIDARI†Y _____ CALENDAR

The following calendar identifies holidays, holy days, feast days, and other events that lend themselves to a focus on global solidarity. It is not intended to be comprehensive, nor is it a calendar for any particular year. Rather, it identifies the date, month, or season when selected events occur on a consistent basis.

World Day of Peace . . . . January 1

National Migration Week . . . . First Week of January

Feast of the Epiphany . . . . January

Collection for the Church in Latin America . . . . January

Collection for the Church in Eastern Europe . . . . Ash Wednesday/Lent

Feast of St. Paul Miki and Companions (Japanese Martyrs) . . . . February 6

Operation Rice Bowl . . . . Lent

American Bishops' Overseas Appeal . . . . Laetare Sunday

Feast of St. Patrick, Patron of Ireland . . . . March 17

Anniversary of the Death of Archbishop Romero . . . . March 23

Feast of Pentecost . . . . Spring

Feast of St. Charles Lwanga and Companions (Ugandan Martyrs) . . . . June 3

Feast of St. Maximillian Kolbe (Killed during the Holocaust) . . . . August 14

Feast of St. Andrew Kim Taegôn, Paul Chông Hasang and Companions (Korean Martyrs) . . . . . . September 20

Respect Life Month . . . . October

World Youth Day . . . . October

Feast of St. Theresa of Lisieux, Patroness of the Missions . . . . October 1

Holy Childhood Day . . . . First Friday of October

World Mission Sunday . . . . Next to the Last Sunday of October

Feast of St. Frances Xavier Cabrini, Patroness of Emigrants . . . . November 13

Anniversary of the Death of Five Jesuits and Two Women in El Salvador . . . . November 16

Anniversary of the Death of Three Church Women in El Salvador . . . . December 2

Feast of St. Francis Xavier, Patron of the Missions . . . . December 3

Feast of Our Lady of Guadalupe . . . . December 12

FACT SHEET

- 35,000 persons die of hunger and its consequences every day around the world.

- More than 80 percent of the world's people live in developing countries. They use just 20 percent of the world's wealth. The remaining 20 percent of the world's people live in industrialized nations and control 80 percent of the world's wealth.

- Women perform two-thirds of the world's work, but receive one-tenth of its income and own less than one-hundredth of its property.

- As of 1995, developing nations owed foreign creditors more than $2 trillion. The cost of providing relief for the twenty nations worst affected by the international debt burden would be $6 billion, less than the cost of one stealth bomber.

- In Uganda, the government spends $3.50 per person annually on health and education and $17.00 per person annually on debt relief.

- The United States ranks first in the world in weapons sold to poor nations, yet near last among industrialized nations in the proportion of resources devoted to development for the poor.

- 26,000 people, mostly civilians, are maimed or killed every year by antipersonnel landmines.

- More than 20 million people worldwide have been displaced due to human conflict or forced relocation. In Bosnia and Herzegovina, one in every two persons has been displaced.

Data cited from Catholic Relief Services, the United Nations, the World Bank, the Catholic Fund for Overseas Development, the Hunger Project, the Vietnam Veterans of America, Oxfam International, Bread for the World, the *1996 World Fact Book*, and the *1996 World Refugee Survey*.

A suffering world must find a place in the pastoral priorities of every Catholic parish. A parish's "catholicity" is illustrated in its willingness to go beyond its own boundaries to extend the Gospel, serve those in need, and work for global justice and peace. This is not a work for a few agencies or one parish committee, but for every believer and every local community of faith. This solidarity is expressed in our prayer and stewardship, how we form our children and invest our resources, and the choices we make at work and in the public arena.

U.S. Catholic Bishops

We are tempted by the illusion of isolationism to turn away from global leadership in an understandable but dangerous preoccupation with the problems of our own communities and nation. In the face of these challenges we see divergent paths. One path is that of indifference, even hostility to global engagement. Another path views the world as simply a global market for the goods and services of the United States. Our faith calls us to a different road—a path of global responsibility and solidarity.

U.S. Catholic Bishops

Our faith challenges us to reach out to those in need, to take on the global status quo and to resist the immorality of isolationism. In one sense, we need to move our Church's concern from strong teaching to creative action. Working together, we can continue to help missionaries preach the Gospel, empower poor people in their own development, help the Church live and grow in lands marked by repression and poverty, and assist countries emerging from authoritarian rule.

U.S. Catholic Bishops

As we approach the great Jubilee, let us rediscover in our time the meaning of the mystical body of Christ. We should mark the new millennium by making our families and local communities of faith signs of genuine solidarity—praying, teaching, preaching, and acting with new urgency and creativity on the international obligations of our faith.

U.S. Catholic Bishops

We have heard the Lord's command, "Love your neighbor as yourself." In our linked and limited world, loving our neighbor has global implications. In faith, we know our neighbors live in Rwanda and Sudan, in East Timor and China, in Bosnia and Central America, as well as across our country and next door. Baptism, confirmation, and continuing participation in the body of Christ calls us to action for "the least among us" without regard for boundaries or borders.

U.S. Catholic Bishops

Solidarity is action on behalf of the one human family, calling us to help overcome the divisions in our world. Solidarity binds the rich to the poor. It makes the free zealous for the cause of the oppressed. It drives the comfortable and secure to take risks for the victims of tyranny and war. It calls those who are strong to care for those who are weak and vulnerable across the spectrum of human life. It opens homes and hearts to those in flight from terror and to migrants whose daily toil supports affluent lifestyles.

U.S. Catholic Bishops

Pope John Paul II sharply challenges the growing gaps between rich and poor nations and between rich and poor within nations. He recognizes the important values of market economics but insists they be guided by the option for the poor and the principle of the global common good. He challenges leaders to respect human life and human rights, to protect workers and the vulnerable. He insists nations halt the arms trade, ban landmines, promote true development, and relieve the crushing burden of international debt.

U.S. Catholic Bishops

We respond very generously when the network news tells us of hurricanes and famines, but how will we help those victimized by the often less visible disasters of poverty caused by structural injustice, such as debt, ethnic conflict, and the arms trade? Our Church and parishes must call us anew to sacrifice and concern for a new generation of children who need food, justice, peace, and the Gospel. A central task for the next century is building families of faith that reach out beyond national boundaries.

U.S. Catholic Bishops

Years ago we raised funds for "pagan babies," cleaned our plates, and prayed after Mass for the conversion of Russia. We didn't have global TV networks or the Internet, but we had a sense of responsibility. Over the years, we have continued this tradition through our missions, our collections for and advocacy on international needs, and our global development programs. We need to acknowledge and renew this traditional Catholic consciousness in a new age of global communications and economic interdependence.

U.S. Catholic Bishops

Through the eyes of faith, the starving child, the believer in jail, and the woman without clean water or health care are not issues, but Jesus in disguise. The human and moral costs of the arms trade, international debt, environmental neglect, and ethnic violence are not abstractions, but tests of our faith. Violence in the Holy Land, tribal combat in Africa, religious persecution, and starvation around the world are not just headlines, but a call to action. As Catholics, we are called to renew the earth, not escape its challenge.

U.S. Catholic Bishops

The call to solidarity is at the heart of Pope John Paul II's leadership. He has insisted that the test of national leadership is how we reach out to defend and enhance the dignity of the poor and vulnerable, at home and around the world. He calls us to defense of all human life and care for God's creation. In his visits to this country, the Holy Father called on our nation to "spare no effort in advancing authentic freedom and in fostering human rights and solidarity."

U.S. Catholic Bishops

Our efforts must begin with fundamental reform of the "structures of violence" that bring suffering and death to the poor. The Catholic community will continue to speak on behalf of increased development assistance, relief from international debt, curbs on the arms trade, and respect for human life and the rights of families. We will continue to oppose population policies that insist on inclusion of abortion among the methods of family planning. Our foreign aid and peacemaking efforts can be reformed and improved, but they cannot be abandoned.

U.S. Catholic Bishops

The Church's teaching on international justice and peace is not simply a mandate for a few large agencies, but a challenge for every believer and every Catholic community of faith.

U.S. Catholic Bishops

Additional Resources and Organizations

There are many resources and organizations to which parishes can turn for additional information on international concerns. The following list provides a sampling of these resources and organizations.

I. Print and Video Resources

A. Global

United States Catholic Conference
3211 Fourth Street, N.E.
Washington, DC 20017-1194
Telephone (toll-free): 800-235-8722
Telephone (Washington metropolitan area):
202-722-8716
Fax: 202-722-8709

Catechism of the Catholic Church for Personal Computers. The complete *Catechism* in an electronic database. No. 5-061, $69.95.

The Challenge of Peace: God's Promise and Our Response. The U.S. bishops' landmark 1983 pastoral on nuclear weapons and the arms race. No. 863-0, 142 pp., $3.95.

Communities of Salt and Light: Reflections on the Social Mission of the Parish. The U.S. bishops' statement for pastors and parish leaders seeking to strengthen parish social ministry. English: No. 701-4, 24 pp. $1.95; Spanish: No. 724-3, 24 pp., $1.95.

Communities of Salt and Light: Parish Resource Manual. Includes the bishops' statement and suggestions for parish action. No. 702-2, 52 pp., $5.95.

Food Policy in a Hungry World: The Links that Bind Us Together. The U.S. bishops' reflection on food and agricultural policy in the light of the gospel. No. 320-5, 36 pp., $1.95.

The Harvest of Justice Is Sown in Peace. The U.S. bishops' most comprehensive statement on ethics and international affairs after the Cold War. English: No. 705-7, 28 pp., $2.95; Spanish: No. 706-5, 28 pp., $2.95.

Peacemaking: Moral and Policy Challenges for a New World. A compendium of articles addressing the religious and moral dimensions of many of the most pressing issues confronting U.S. foreign policy today. No. 682-4, 368 pp., $19.95.

Political Responsibility: Proclaiming the Gospel of Life, Protecting the Least Among Us, and Pursuing the Common Good. Looks at the role of the individual Catholic and the role of the Church in political life. Provides an overview of church teaching on key domestic and international issues. English: No. 5-043, 40 pp., $1.75; Spanish: No. 5-044, 40 pp., $1.75.

Relieving Third World Debt: A Call for Co-responsibility, Justice, and Solidarity. Considers the impact of Third World debt on the poor. No. 311-6, 52 pp., $3.50.

Renewing the Earth: An Invitation to Reflection and Action on Environment in Light of Catholic Social Teaching. The U.S. bishops' reflection on environmental justice. No. 468-6, 20 pp.

Sowing the Weapons of War: A Pastoral Reflection on the Arms Trade and Landmines. The U.S. Bishops' review of the post-Cold War arms trade. No. 5-028, 12 pp., $1.50.

USCC Department of Social Development and World Peace
3211 Fourth Street, N.E.
Washington, DC 20017
Telephone: 202-541-3195
Fax: 202-541-3339
E-mail: rfowler@nccbuscc.org

Issue and Resource Mailings. Include complimentary copies of conference justice and peace documents; updates on social justice issues and legislation; legislative "Action Alerts"; resource listings, and more. Subscription: $30.00 for eight mailings per year.

Catholic Relief Services—USCC
209 West Fayette Street
Baltimore, MD 21201
Telephone: 410-625-2220, ext. 3214
Fax: 410-234-3183
E-mail: wokeefe@catholicrelief.org

CRS: The Relief of Suffering. A video that provides a brief introduction to the mission and work of CRS (viewing time: 9 minutes, 20 seconds). Free.

Materials for Operation Rice Bowl (See description on page 18.) Includes these four pieces: (1) Rice Bowl—The rice bowl is the primary symbol of hunger and hardship faced by the world's poor. Participants contribute alms in a cardboard rice bowl; the alms are then used to reach out to the disadvantaged. (2) Home Calendar Guide—The centerpiece of the program in the home, the calendar provides families with daily opportunities to enrich their Lenten experience and learn about the lives of people in the developing world. (3) Educator's Guide—Suitable for use in religious education programs, Catholic schools, and youth ministry, this guide includes lesson plans and hands-on activities. (4) Video: *A Child's Perspective*—Designed to be shown at parish gatherings or school programs to explain how a group can make a difference through Operation Rice Bowl (viewing time: 8 minutes, 39 seconds). To learn more about Operation Rice Bowl or to order free materials, call 800- 222-0025.

Materials for Work of Human Hands (See description on page 19.) Includes these four pieces: (1) Easy Steps to Work of Human

Hands Planning Guide—Provides five easy steps that will enable any coordinator to plan an event to support the Work of Human Hands project. (2) Catalog—Displays the exquisite items available through the Work of Human Hands Project. Items are made available for individual or bulk purchase. A variety of items are available, all of which are truly breathtaking. (3) Lesson Plan—Includes themes, objectives, motivational stories, and procedures for active participation. (4) Video: *A Vision of Human Dignity*—Designed to provide people with an opportunity to become involved with the lives of the poor in the developing world (viewing time: 9 minutes, 30 seconds; 1996). For more information or to order a catalogue or any of the above materials, call 800-685-7572.

Preaching a Global Gospel. A booklet that provides a homily/reflection program centered on the experiences of seminarians who have traveled to CRS locations overseas through the Global Fellows Program. For more information, contact the Church Outreach Department at 800-235-2772. Free.

Putting Life Before Debt. A position paper and advocacy guide from two global networks of Catholic relief and development agencies: International Co-operation for Development and Solidarity (CIDSE) and Caritas Internationalis (CI). The paper outlines a Catholic position on international debt and proposes actions for canceling the debt in light of the Jubilee Year 2000. Free.

B. Issues

1. Children and Youth

United States Catholic Conference

Who Are My Sisters and Brothers? A Catholic Educational Guide for Understanding and Welcoming Immigrants and Refugees. An educational resource for Catholic schools and religious education programs (K-12), youth retreats, teacher/catechist in-service, and parent/other adult sessions. The guide provides lesson plans, readings, games, graphics, exercises and other activities, and a list of resources. No. 5-006, 280 pp., $14.95.

Catholic Relief Services

Materials for Food Fast (See description on page 19.) Includes these two pieces: (1) Food Fast Brochure—This simple brochure provides individuals and communities with the opportunity to participate in an organized Food Fast. (2) Coordinator's Manual—This manual provides educators with a planning calendar for the supervisor, a school implementation plan, a complete schedule of activities, and worksheets for use during the Food Fast Program. For more information or to order free materials, call 800-222-0025.

The Holy Childhood Association

1720 Massachusetts Avenue, N.W.
Washington, DC 20036
Telephone: 202-775-8637
Fax: 202-429-2987

Seasonal Appeals. Educational materials for elementary school children, including seasonal appeals for Halloween, Advent, and Lent, and intercultural education materials. Free.

The Columban Fathers' Mission Education Office

St. Columbans, NE 68056
Telephone: 402-291-1920

Come and See and *Challenged and Empowered*. Mission education curriculum materials for elementary, middle school, and high school students in schools and religious education programs. Adult catechetical programs are also available. $40.00.

Your Diocesan Director of the Propagation of the Faith or Propagation of the Faith National Office

366 Fifth Avenue
New York, NY 10001
Telephone: 800-431-2222
Website: www.propfaith.org

Becoming Disciples: A Faith Journey. A video focusing on the personal experiences of high school students and seminarians who shared a two-week mission experience in Ecuador. Discussion and study guide included (viewing time: 23 minutes). $9.95.

Connections. A video designed for students in secondary schools and religious education programs, that provides an understandable theology of mission and examples of ways that high school students can participate in the Church's mission work. Discussion and study guide included (viewing time: 15 minutes). $9.95.

On Mission. A video discussing the theology of mission and organized around the themes of prayer, personal sacrifice, financial sacrifice, and service to others. Focuses on the work of young Jesuit International Volunteers in Belize, Central America. Discussion guide included (viewing time: 20 minutes; 1993). $9.95.

Witness. A video featuring young people talking about their mission experience in Haiti: why they went, what they saw, what their time there meant in their lives and for their faith (viewing time 22 minutes). $9.95

Maryknoll World Productions

P.O. Box 308
Maryknoll, NY 10545-0308
Telephone: 800-227-8523
Fax: 914-945-0670

Banking on Life and Debt. A 30-minute video documentary showing how people in Ghana, Brazil, and the Philippines are trapped by their governments' outstanding debt owed to the World Bank and International Monetary Fund. $14.95.

Children of the Earth. A video series including "Asia Close-Up," focusing on Japan and Cambodia, and "Africa Close-Up," focusing on Egypt and Tanzania. $16.95.

The Ties That Bind. A one-hour video program in English or Spanish looking at the human drama behind the current debate over U.S. immigration policy. Three twenty-minute segments are designed to facilitate classroom or group discussion. $19.95.

The World Through Kids' Eyes. A series of six video short stories providing a unique insight into the reality and dreams of children from six countries: the Philippines, Peru, Brazil, The United States, India, and South Africa. $29.95.

2. Immigrants and Refugees

United States Catholic Conference

One Family Under God: A Statement of the U.S. Bishops' Committee on Migration. A statement on immigration and other public policy issues. English: No. 5-270, 28 pp., $1.95; Spanish: No. 5-271, 28 pp., $1.95.

Who Are My Sisters and Brothers? Reflections on Understanding and Welcoming Immigrants and Refugees. A collection of short essays on the situation of refugees today; a theological reflection on immigration; the human rights of people regarding migration; the history of Catholics and immigrants in America; U.S. immigration and refugee policy; and immigrant families in cultural transition. No. 5-057, 54 pp., $6.95.

Who Are My Sisters and Brothers? Understanding and Welcoming Immigrants and Refugees. A brief video history of immigration to the United States, followed by examples of three parishes that are working with immigrants and refugees. Discussion guide included. No. 5-053, 29 minutes, $19.95.

Pastoral Care of Migrants and Refugees
USCC Migration and Refugee Services
3211 Fourth Street, N.E.
Washington, DC 20017-1194
Telephone: 202-541-3230
Fax: 202-541-3351
E-mail: pcmr@nccbuscc.org

National Migration Week Resources. A variety of ready-to-use resources to help parishes celebrate National Migration Week. Free.

PCMR Resource Briefs. Periodic publications covering a range of topics of interest to those working with immigrants and refugees. Free.

Jesuit Conference Office of Social Ministries
1616 P Street, N.W.
Suite 400
Washington, DC 20036-1405
Telephone: 202-462-7008

The Lifeboat and the Banquet: Two Images for Contemplating Immigrant Human Rights. Luis Tampe, SJ. Booklet that contrasts national immigration policies with Catholic social teaching. 14 pp. $2.00.

3. Mission

United States Catholic Conference

Celebrating "To the Ends of the Earth": An Anniversary Statement on World Mission. English: No. 5-038, 20 pp., $1.50; Spanish: No. 5-039, 20 pp., $1.50.

Propagation of the Faith National Office
366 Fifth Avenue
New York, NY 10001
Telephone: 800-431-2222
Website: www.propfaith.org

Alone with Our Lord: A Meditation on Our Universal Call to Mission. Rev. Eugene La Verdiere, SSS. Prayers, Scripture readings, and meditations on the universal call to mission. 15 pp. $0.20.

In the Presence of Christ: A Meditation on Our Universal Call to Mission. Rev. Eugene La Verdiere, SSS. A group prayer service on the theme of the universal call to mission to be used during the exposition of the Blessed Sacrament. 15 pp. $0.20.

Lay People in the Mission of the Church. Rev. Eugene La Verdiere, SSS. Reflections based on *Christifideles Laici* that explore the missionary aspect of Christian life as lived by the lay person. 15 pp. $0.40.

MISSION Magazine. A quarterly publication that offers news of the local churches in the missions and provides ideas for Catholics to reach out through prayer and sacrifice to help our brothers and sisters in the missions.

Mission in the Catechism of the Catholic Church. Rev. Eugene La Verdiere, SSS. Discusses how missionary responsibility is a major and integrating theme that permeates the entire *Catechism of the Catholic Church*. 27 pp. $0.40.

Ordained for the Universal Church. Rev. Eugene La Verdiere, SSS. Focuses on the missionary dimension of the priesthood as presented by Pope John Paul II in *Pastores Dabo Vobis.* 30 pp. $0.40.

Why Catholics Don't Evangelize and Why They Must. Rev. Avery Dulles, SJ. Discusses the history of evangelization in the Church, focusing on the theme of the "new evangelization" in Pope John Paul II's teaching. 27 pp. $0.25.

World Mission Sunday Materials. The World Mission Sunday Diocesan Director's Planner contains tips, suggestions, and sample letters to parish organizations, priests, and directors of campus ministries (among others). Also available are a leaflet (2 pp.) describing World Mission Sunday, a Priest's Guide (4 pp.) Liturgy Suggestions (2 pp.), and posters for parish use. Sent to director free.

You Are Called to Be Missionary: A Mission Spirituality for All Catholics. Rev. Eugene La Verdiere, SSS. Discusses the relationship of discipleship, Church, sacraments, prayer, and sacrifice to mission. 32 pp. $0.40.

U.S. Catholic Mission Association
3029 Fourth Street, N.E.
Washington, DC 20017-1102
Telephone: 202-832-3112
Fax: 202-832-3688
E-mail: uscma@igc.org

U.S. Catholic Mission Handbook: Mission Inventory 1996-1997. Statistics summary of foreign missions. 56 pp. $5.00 (USA), $8.00 (International).

C. Regions

1. Africa

Africa Faith and Justice Network
P.O. Box 29378
Washington, DC 20017
Telephone: 202-832-3412

Moral Imperatives for Addressing Structural Adjustment and Economic Reform Measures. A seven-part series identifying moral values to be used as the basis for dialogue about economic and other social reforms. 10 pp. Free.

2. Central and Eastern Europe

Office to Aid the Catholic Church in Central and Eastern Europe
National Conference of Catholic Bishops
3211 Fourth Street, N.E.
Washington, DC 20017-1194
Telephone: 202-541-3400

Out of the Darkness. Provides a brief video history of the Church in Central and Eastern Europe and looks at the conditions of the people and the Church since the transition to democracy in the region (viewing time: 15 minutes). Free.

3. Latin America

United States Catholic Conference

Sharing Faith Across the Hemisphere. An overview of the history of the relationship between the Church in the United States and Latin America since 1961, discussing the theology of mission and evangelization, conditions in Latin America today, and examples of how dioceses, religious communities, parishes, and Catholic colleges and universities are working with their Latin American sisters and brothers. English book: No. 5-015, 320 pp., $19.95; Spanish book: No. 5-125, 336 pp., $19.95; English video (discussion and study guide included): No. 5-016, 28 minutes, $19.95; Spanish video: No. 5-126, 28 minutes, $19.95.

Secretariat for Latin America
National Conference of Catholic Bishops
3211 Fourth Street, N.E.
Washington, DC 20017-1194
Telephone: 202-541-3050
Website: www.nccbuscc.org/latinamerica

Una Vista. A newsletter published twice yearly by the Secretariat for Latin America to inform Catholics in the United States about the Church in Latin America. Subscriptions are free.

4. Middle East

United States Catholic Conference

Toward Peace in the Middle East: Perspectives, Principles, and Hopes. The U.S. bishops' review of leaders' responsibilities in the cause of peace. No. 325-6, 52 pp., $2.95.

Catholic Near East Welfare Association
1011 First Avenue
New York, NY 10022-4195
Telephone: 212-826-1480

Catholic Near East. The bimonthly magazine of the Catholic Near East Welfare Association; Annual subscription: $10.00.

Resource materials on the Middle East are also available, including an annotated listing of periodicals, videocassettes, books, children's books, educational materials, and organizations

II. Organizations and Programs

A. National Conference of Catholic Bishops/ United States Catholic Conference

Apostleship of the Sea in the United States
Telephone: 202-541-3065, ext. 3226

Assists seafarers around the world to meet their basic needs: a safe work environment, a just contract, a safe haven while in port, spiritual renewal, and communication with loved ones back home.

Catholic Campaign to Ban Landmines
Social Development and World Peace
Telephone: 202-541-3199
Fax: 202-541-3339
E-mail: landmines@nccbuscc.org

A coalition including the United States Catholic Conference, the military archdiocese, Catholic Relief Services, missionary societies, religious communities, refugee groups, and many other Catholic organizations that is urging effective, strong U.S. leadership to ban the use, production, stockpiling, and sale of these indiscriminate killers. The campaign has available a packet that includes a fact sheet and resource list on landmines, suggestions for pastoral and liturgy committees, social concerns committees, and schools and directors of religious education.

Catholic Campaign to Relieve Debt
Social Development and World Peace
Telephone: 202-541-3153
Fax: 202-541-3339
E-mail: bkohnen@nccbuscc.org
Website: http://www.j2000usa.org.

A member of the Jubilee 2000 USA coalition, which includes Catholic organizations, religious communities, economic and environmental justice groups, and many others. The coalition is part of a worldwide movement to relieve the crushing international debt of impoverished countries by the new millennium. For more information on Jubilee 2000 USA, contact the coordinator at 202-783-3566.

Environmental Justice Program
Telephone: 202-541-3160
Fax: 202-541-3339
E-mail: jortman-fouse@nccbuscc.org

Promotes environmental justice and care for creation and offers a variety of parish packets, videos, small grants, and other resources to help the Catholic community respond to the bishops' statement on the environment, *Renewing the Earth.*

Pastoral Care of Migrants and Refugees
USCC Migration and Refugee Services Unit
Telephone: 202-541-3230

Provides assistance to parishes and other Catholic organizations to welcome newcomers. Serves as a clearinghouse of information, offers leadership development programs, and produces language- and culture-appropriate liturgical and religious education materials.

B. Other Organizations

Amnesty International, USA
322 Eighth Avenue
New York, NY 10001
Telephone: 212-807-8400

Pursues human rights worldwide and offers a variety of resources including parish tools to create a letter writing advocacy program addressing global human rights concerns.

Bread for the World
1100 Wayne Avenue, Suite 1000
Silver Spring, MD 20910
Telephone: 301-608-2400

Provides a range of global education and advocacy resources to help parishioners work for the alleviation of global poverty and hunger.

Catholic Legal Immigration Network, Inc. (CLINIC)
National Office
Theological College, 1st Floor
401 Michigan Avenue, N.E.
Washington, DC 20017
Telephone: 202-635-2556

Provides information on mass citizen workshops, volunteer training, and immigration-related employment discrimination. Does not provide direct legal services.

Catholic Migrant Farmworker Network
1915 University Drive
Boise, ID 83706
Telephone: 208-384-1879
Fax: 208-384-1879

Provides a quarterly newsletter, a video, and a variety of bilingual booklets on the sacraments and other faith-related topics specifically designed for migrant farmworkers and their families.

Center of Concern
3700 13th Street, N.E.
Washington, DC 20017
Telephone: 202-635-2757
Fax: 202-832-9494
E-mail: coc@igc.apc.org

Promotes social analysis, theological reflection, policy advocacy, and public education on issues of global development, domestic/global links, and just international finance and trade. The center also produces a newsletter, *Center Focus,* and has available a number of publications and videos.

Conference of Major Superiors of Men's Institutes
8808 Cameron Street
Silver Spring, MD 20910
Telephone: 301-588-4030
Fax: 301-587-4575
E-mail: humanrightsedu@cmsm.org

Offers a program of human rights education to help celebrate the fiftieth anniversary of the *Universal Declaration of Human Rights*. Their *Human Rights Education Handbook* is intended for parishes, schools, and other community groups, and it includes educational materials, resources, information on Catholic social teaching, and group exercises.

Ethics and Public Policy Center
1015 15th Street, N.W., Suite 900
Washington, DC 20005
Telephone: 202-682-1200
Fax: 202-408-0632

Conducts a program of research, writing, publications, and conferences to encourage debate on domestic and foreign policy issues among religious, educational, academic, business, political, and other leaders.

Free the Children
16 Thornbank Road
Thornhill, Ontario
Canada - L4J 2A2
Telephone: 905-881-0863
Fax: 905-881-1849
E-mail: freechild@clo.com
Website: www.freethechildren.org

An organization of children and young people ages eight to eighteen working to end child labor and child abuse. Offers a variety of resources and information.

Freedom House
1319 18th Street, N.W.
Washington, DC 20036
Telephone: 202-296-5101
Fax: 202-296-5078

A foundation dedicated to documenting the violation of human rights around the world. Produces a variety of materials on human rights abuses in different countries.

Haiti Parish Twinning Program
208 Leake Avenue
Nashville, TN 37205
Telephone: 615-356-5999
Fax: 615-352-5114
E-mail: Haiti.Program@worldnet.att.net

Promotes twinning relationships between parishes in the United States and parishes in Haiti. Publishes a newsletter, *Haitian Connection.*

Inter-Church Committee on Northern Ireland (ICNI)
c/o Gerard Powers
Telephone: 202-541-3199
Fax: 202-541-3339
E-mail: gpowers@nccbuscc.org

Brings together four religious groups—The United States Catholic Conference, the Catholic Bishops of the Armagh Province (Northern Ireland), the Presbyterian Church, USA, and the Presbyterian Church, Ireland—to facilitate closer relations, discuss issues of mutual concern in Northern Ireland, and support parish activities, including:
Ecumenical Sister Parish Program. Designed to bring together Catholic and Presbyterian congregations in the United States and to help them establish an exchange program with Catholic and Presbyterian congregations in Northern Ireland.

Summer Institute on Northern Ireland. A biennial tour that provides two dozen Americans with an in-depth introduction to the conflict in Northern Ireland.

Speaking Tours. Tours to U.S. parishes, congregations, and other places by ecumenical teams from Northern Ireland in order to edu-cate Americans about the conflict and the efforts of the churches to promote peace, justice, and reconciliation.

National Council of Catholic Women
1275 K Street, N.W.
Suite 975
Washington, DC 20005
Telephone: 202-682-0334
Fax: 202-682-0338

Offers a variety of programs that help parishes, families, and individuals assist those in need around the world, including:

Works of Peace: Madonna Plan (education/development for women), Help-A-Child (health/education), Water for Life (water/land/sustainable development);

Works of Reconciliation: Refugee Women Emergency Fund.

Also publishes *Catholic Woman,* a bimonthly magazine.

Oxfam International
1511 K Street, N.W.
Suite 640
Washington, DC 20005
Telephone: 202-393-5333

Provides information on Third World debt, poverty, Africa, and hunger. Active in lobbying the World Bank and International Monetary Fund for international debt relief.

Pax Christi USA
532 West Eighth Street
Erie, PA 16502
Telephone: 814-453-4955
Fax: 814-452-4784
E-mail: paxchristi@igc.apc.org

Promotes prayer, study, and action on behalf of peace and justice and works to build solidarity locally, nationally, and internationally. Also produces a quarterly newspaper, periodic mailings on peace and justice issues, and materials for prayer, reflection, and education for use by individuals, the parish, and the classroom.

Religious Task Force on Central America and Mexico
3053 Fourth Street, N.E.
Washington, DC 20117-1102
Telephone: 202-529-0441

A faith-based network of persons working for new relationships between the people of North and Latin America based on respect for the dignity and freedom of the region's poor and indigenous peoples. Publishes *Central America/Mexico Report* ($20/year) and parish materials for the annual commemoration of Archbishop Romero (March) and the four missionary women and the UCA Jesuits (November-December) killed in El Salvador.

Washington Office on Latin America (WOLA)
400 C Street, N.E.
Washington, DC 20002
Telephone: 202-544-8045
Fax: 202-546-5288

Promotes policies that advance human rights, democracy, and social justice in Latin America. Serves as a bridge connecting different networks—the human rights and foreign policy communities, academic think-tanks, and religiously based "solidarity"groups—with each other and with policy makers. Publishes numerous reports and a Spanish-language newsletter.

Resources Available from the U.S. Bishops

Sowing Weapons of War
*A Pastoral Reflection on the Arms Trade
and Landmines*
The U.S. bishops affirm the duty to avoid war and
promote peace; the right of legitimate defense; the
principle of sufficiency; and the inadequacy of economic justifications for arms transfers.
No. 5-028, 12 pp., $1.50

Catholic Campaign to Ban Landmines
Brochure
Eight-page brochure outlines the reasons the
Catholic Church is seeking a ban on landmines.
Includes action steps that Catholics can take and
brief facts about landmines.
No. 5-223, package of 100, $12.00

Catholic Campaign to Ban Landmines
Poster
The poster has compelling photographs of one
landmine survivor with his child and of Pope John
Paul II meeting with another landmine survivor.
No. 5-224, $2.00

Peacemaking
Moral and Policy Challenges for a New World
Addresses the religious and moral dimensions of
many of the most pressing issues confronting U.S.
foreign policy today. Contributors include the late
Joseph Cardinal Bernardin, Zbigniew Brzezinski,
and George Weigel. Edited by Gerard F. Powers,
Drew Christiansen, SJ, and Robert T. Hennemeyer.
No. 682-4, 368 pp., $19.95

The Harvest of Justice Is Sown in Peace
*A Reflection of the National Conference of Catholic
Bishops on the Tenth Anniversary of "The
Challenge of Peace"*
The U. S. bishops address the just-war theory,
humanitarian intervention, deterrence, conscien-
tious objection, and the development of peoples.
English: No. 705-7, 28 pp., $2.95
Spanish: No. 706-5, 28 pp., $2.95

The Challenge of Peace
God's Promise and Our Response
The powerful, thought provoking 1983 pastoral of
the U.S. Catholic bishops on nuclear weapons and
the arms race. Ideal for use in schools, personal
reflection, and active ministry.
No. 863-0, 142 pp., $3.95

Communities of Salt and Light
Reflections on the Social Mission of the Parish
Bishops' statement for pastors and parish leaders
presents seven elements of the social mission of
parishes as a framework for planning and assess-
ing that ministry.
English: No. 701-4, 24 pp., $1.95
Spanish: No. 724-3, 24 pp., $1.95

**Communities of Salt and Light:
Parish Resource Manual**
Provides the text, assessment tools, models, and a
variety of resources for parishes to integrate
Catholic social teaching into every aspect of parish
life. From the U.S. bishops' Department of Social
Development and World Peace.
No. 702-2, 52 pp., $5.95

Salt and Light (Videotape)
Outlines the challenges of the bishops' statement
on the social mission of the parish, and ways
parishes can respond. From the U.S. bishops.
No. 703-0, 14 minutes, $24.95

Political Responsibility
*Proclaiming the Gospel of Life, Protecting the Least
Among Us, and Pursuing the Common Good*
Includes the Church's position on issues such as
capital punishment, education, euthanasia, family
life, the environment, immigration, and the mass
media.
English: No. 5-043, 40 pp., $1.75
Spanish: No. 5-044, 40 pp., $1.75

A Call to Political Responsibility
Proclaiming the Gospel of Life, Protecting the Least Among Us, and Pursuing the Common Good
This two-color brochure summarizes the statement on *Political Responsibility* and includes questions regarding the role of citizens in enriching the democratic life of the nation.
English: No. 5-045, $0.35
Spanish: No. 5-046, $0.35

Political Responsibility (Videotape)
An ideal resource for use by committees and parish councils, as well as in the classroom. From the U.S. bishops, the video includes a user's guide.
No. 5-048, 17 minutes, $14.95

Food Policy in a Hungry World
The Links That Bind Us Together
The U.S. bishops examine the plight of the more than one-half billion people in the world who live with hunger and reflects on what food and agricultural policy is needed in light of Gospel and Christian commitment.
No. 320-5, 36 pp., $1.95

Relieving Third World Debt
A Call for Co-responsibility, Justice, and Solidarity
Considers the impact of Third World debt on the poor. From the U.S. bishops' Administrative Board.
No. 311-6, 52 pp., $3.50

No.	Title	Quantity	List Price	Total
5-028	Sowing Weapons of War		$ 1.50	
5-223	Catholic Campaign to Ban Landmines: Brochure (pkg. of 100)		12.00	
5-224	Catholic Campaign to Ban Landmines: Poster		2.00	
682-4	Peacemaking: Moral and Policy Challenges for a New World		19.95	
705-7	The Harvest of Justice Is Sown in Peace		2.95	
706-5	The Harvest of Justice Is Sown in Peace (Spanish)		2.95	
863-0	The Challenge of Peace		2.95	
701-4	Communities of Salt and Light		1.95	
724-3	Communities of Salt and Light (Spanish)		1.95	
702-2	Communities of Salt and Light: Parish Resource Manual		5.95	
703-0	Salt and Light (Videotape)		24.95	
5-043	Political Responsibility		1.75	
5-044	Political Responsibility (Spanish)		1.75	
5-045	A Call to Political Responsibility		0.35	
5-046	A Call to Political Responsibility (Spanish)		0.35	
5-048	Political Responsibility (Videotape)		14.95	
320-5	Food Policy in a Hungry World		1.95	
311-6	Relieving Third World Debt		3.50	

Date _____

Customer Number _____
Customer Name _____
Organization _____
Office _____
Street Address _____
City State Zip _____
Daytime Telephone Number ( ) _____

❏ Check/money order enclosed in the amount of $_____. Please make checks/money orders payable (in U.S. dollars) to *USCC Publishing Services.*

❏ Charge my ❏ MasterCard ❏ VISA
Card Account Number _____
Expiration Date _____
Cardholder's Signature _____

❏ Bill me. *Orders sent without a customer number cannot be billed.*

First total _____
*Discount - _____
Second total _____
Washington, DC, residents: add 5.75% tax + _____
Net Total _____
**Shipping and Handling Charge + _____
GRAND TOTAL _____

F005-0198

* *Discount*: Subtract 20% of first total if customer number is listed in the address portion and full payment by check/money order/credit card is enclosed.

** *Shipping and Handling Charge*: Add 10% of Net Total ($3.00 minimum) on orders sent to addresses in the United States, Canada, and Mexico. Add 15% of Net Total ($5.00 minimum) on orders sent to all other addresses.

Mail your order to: Publishing Services, United States Catholic Conference, 3211 Fourth Street NE, Washington DC 20017-1194. Or fax your order to (202) 722-8709. You may also phone orders to (800) 235-8722. Visit the U.S. bishops' internet site at www.nccbuscc.org.